MW00904111

Savages and Saints

Life and Love on the New Guinea Mission Fields

by

Leon and Theophila Philippi

as told by Malcolm Smith

Savages and Saints, life and love on the New Guinea mission fields

© Malcolm Smith, 2020

Leon and Theophila Philippi are recognized as joint authors, with Malcolm Smith as secondary author.

ISBN: 9781654850586

Imprint: Independently published

Photos courtesy of Rev. Leon Philippi.

Cover photograph: church attendance in the Bena Bena district.

Chapters

New Guinea Terminology

The pronunciation of place names and personal names will, of course, differ according to the local language, but in general, one can observe the following rules, unless stated otherwise: Stress is on the first syllable.

a   as in *father*, but usually shorter, more like the *u* in *bud*.

e   as in *bed*

i   as in *bin*

o   as in *body*

u   as in *ruse* or *bull*

ai   as in *aisle*

au   rhymes with *cow*

Glossary

asgras: a cluster of tanget grass stuck into a Highland man's belt to cover his buttocks (English "arse grass")

bilum: string bag. Men use long handled bags which can be slung over the shoulder, while women carry them on the back, with the handles looped over the forehead.

garamut: a large drum, constructed from a hollowed-out tree trunk, with a slot cut in the top. It rests upon the ground, and is beaten with a wooden club.

grile: [*grill-* ay] ringworm

haus kiap: a house set aside for the use of the kiap on his visits

haus kuk: [house cook] exterior kitchen (literally, "cook house")

haus meri: a maid. *Haus* = "house", and is pronounced the same. *Meri* = "woman" (Often incorrectly written "Mary", it appears to have been borrowed from a Melanesian language, rather than the English Christian name.)

kanaka / bush kanaka: [ka-*nack*-a] uncivilised person, a savage. Considered offensive. (From Hawaiian for "human being". This word was brought back from Captain Cook's last voyage, and became the regular English term for a Melanesian.)

kaukau: sweet potato

kiap: [*kee*-up] a colonial official fulfilling the role of patrol officer, policeman, magistrate, tax collector, and general administrator. The kiaps were the backbone of the colonial administration, and the face of the administration most often seen in remote areas. (from German *Kapitän*, captain)

kina: [*kee*-na] the lustrous mother-of-pearl of the gold lip oyster (*Pinctada maxima*), as large as a dinner plate, used for ornaments, and as a form of money. Independent PNG's currency is now called the kina.

konda: lawyer vine (*Smilax australis*) – a prickly vine up to 8 metres long, whose small thorns tend to catch onto clothing and bare skin, with unpleasant results.

kunai: blady grass (*Imperata cylindrica*), a grass ½ – 3 metres in height, with edges made sharp by embedded silica, and able to cut the skin.

kundu: tom-tom, or hand held drum, made out of wood, with an hourglass shape, one end open and the other end covered with lizard skin. The gum of the breadfruit tree is used to attach the skin, and a dob of the gum serves to tune it.

kwila: [*quee*-la] a termite-resistant hardwood timber of the mangrove tree, *Intsia bijuga*, known in north

Queensland as scrub mahogany. It is endangered in much of southeast Asia due to logging, and is the official tree of Guam.

laplap / lavalava: a sarong or loincloth: a strip of cloth wrapped around the waist and reaching partway down the calf, worn by men in the coastal districts.

limbum: (1) the black palm, *Caryota* sp., related to the toddy palm, the timber of which is used for weapons and flooring.

(2) the areca palm, *Cyrtostachys sp.*, whose bark is used for flooring and sometimes the walls of houses, and whose flower sheath converts into mats, baskets, matting, and wrapping.

luluai: a government appointed village headman. He wore a special cap and badge as his insignia. (from Kuanua, the language of the Tolais on the Gazelle Peninsula, *luai-ne*, first)

Miti Binang: [*mitt*-ee *bee*-nung] "The Gospel Story" or course of Bible lessons taught in the indigenous churches. (*Miti* is a Kâte word used to translate the term, "gospel", but actually implies the state of being in harmony or right condition.)

mumu / mum: a form of cooking by burying food on top of a layer of hot stones or embers – especially used during singsings

Pidgin: the lingua franca of the Territory of New Guinea, introduced by traders in the 19th century, based on a simplified English vocabulary, with additions from German and Melanesian languages. In the language itself it is called *Tok Pisin* ("Talk Pidgin"). The name is a Chinese attempt at pronouncing "business", and it was originally a "business language" between English speaking traders and Cantonese. The immigration of

Chinese labourers to German New Guinea may have helped spread the language.

pitpit: a tall grass (*Setaria* sp.) used as an ornamental plant in the U.S., especially Hawaii, where it is known as "palm grass", but used as a food source in Papua New Guinea.

pukpuk: a crocodile - also, ringworm, from the crocodile-like scaliness of the skin presented by widespread infection.

sanggoma: black magic, sorcery (unlikely to be related to the similar Nguni word, *sangoma* for a South African witchdoctor)

singsing: a party or festival

tanget: (*tung*-et) a shrub, *Cordyline fruticosa* of the asparagus family, up to 4 metres in height, whose leaves, 30 – 60 cm long, are used for various purposes. In English called cabbage palm, or good luck plant, among other names.

taro: the Polynesian name for *Colocasia esculenta*, a crop with edible roots superficially resembling those of sweet potato, and edible leaves similar to those of the ornamental "elephant ear". It is a staple food in Oceania, and was even consumed in the Roman Empire, where it was imported from Egypt. It is likely that it was first domesticated in New Guinea.

tultul: the luluai's assistant

Chapter 1
The Little Farm on the Prairie
Leon's Story

Yes, you can teach an old dog new tricks. I am connected to the internet by broadband. My relatives and former classmates on the other side of the world communicate with me by e-mail. My lifetime hobby of photography is being updated, and I am in the process of digitalising all my old photos. But I draw the line at mobile phones. The last one I allowed near me blew my hearing aid. However, I have to acknowledge that a great many younger people regard them as an absolutely essential accessory. One sees them constantly chatting or texting, occasionally taking photos if they have nothing else better to do. Sometimes the camera can be used to permit them to communicate face to face as well as voice to voice. Added to all this, the up-to-date mobile phone appears to come with internet connection, sports channel, facilities for saving and playing music and/or films, and possibly a GPS with road map. No doubt by the time you read this, several other overpriced and unnecessary applications will have been added.

How can anyone raised in this atmosphere imagine what it was like to be born on a farm in Nebraska more than ninety years ago?

I don't suppose, for example, that the mobile phone generation knows what a "party line" was, so I had better explain. When telephones were first introduced to rural areas, it was not economical to connect each home direct to the interchange. Instead, homes were linked in a series on the same line. When the phone rang (in those days, phones rang, instead of chirped), you knew whether it was for you by the number of rings. If you were busy, or you believed in minding your own business, then you did not pick up the receiver to eavesdrop into somebody else's conversation. But, human nature being what it is, this rule of good manners was honoured as much in the breach as in the observance. And, obviously the person whose calls were the most newsworthy was the local doctor. Thus, it was the phone call my father made to Dr Saylor that freezing winter night that announced my impending arrival into the world.

Let us be clear about one thing: despite my surname, I am not Greek. My distant ancestors were supposed to be, but not me. Family tradition, for what it is worth, tells of four Greek brothers who spread out across Europe to seek their fortunes. One branch of the family moved into Spain, and then crossed the Atlantic. Well, that's the story, but a brief surf on the net will reveal that Philippi is really a Latinised German surname, the genitive of "Philipp" and thus "Philipp's son". In any case, by the time Fred Philippi married Laura Springer, they had firmly ensconced themselves in the German speaking Lutheran communities of the U.S. In a dialect similar to "Pennsylavia Dutch", German was our language at home until I reached my teens, by which time it was noticed that little sister Lois was stuttering in her attempts to speak English at school. From then on, English was the home language.

There may even be an aristocratic, perhaps royal, contribution to my lineage, but if so, it is marred by the bar sinister. My paternal grandmother, Sophie came to America as in infant, in the arms of her father, who had belonged to the staff of one of the noble houses of Germany. The identity of the mother, however, was never revealed. Strangely enough, though, regular Christmas presents of expensive clothing and toys continued to arrive from the old country for Sophie until she came of age, producing much resentment among her siblings. The natural conclusion was that her father had got pregnant someone far too high in the social order to permit marriage, and this was the simplest method to avoid scandal.

In any case, when I was born on the morning of January 19, 1927, I had already been preceded seven years before by my brother, Ernest, and just over three years before by my sister, Elda, who was slightly mentally retarded due to rubella exposure in the womb. Almost eight years later, as a late gift from above and, I am told, after a miscarriage, Lois arrived to make up the quartet.

So it was that my earliest memories are of the weatherboard farmhouse on Highway 4, two miles west of Highway 81, which led to Bruning, Nebraska, a further two miles away. Seldom did an automobile grace that gravel highway; horse and buggy carried our family, and most of our neighbours, ploughing ruts deep in the mud and slush when the rains arrived.

A feather bed in the attic was shared by my brother and me. Meanwhile, down below, on cold winter nights, the fire in the stove would be banked down to save it from dying, and a hole in the ceiling allowed the heat to rise into our bedroom. Just the same, in later years, when we had moved to a new farm, we would often awake to discover the corner of our bed decked with snowflakes, blown in through the window during the night. There were also a few times – I forget how many – when we woke up in darkness and watched in awe as the aurora borealis, the northern lights, performed their magic dance against the Nebraskan sky.

Santa Claus never visited our house at Christmas; he was just not part of our tradition. Instead, the presents were simply placed around the tree by friends and relatives, who made no secret of their identity.

Winters were bad. Snow could pile up in deep drifts, and the temperature could fall to 25 degrees below zero. That's in the old Fahrenheit scale; in Celsius, it would be 32 below. Dad would place storm windows over the standard windows to seal out the cold and the snow. As the cattle and horses still needed to drink from the stock tank, ten feet in diameter and two feet deep, one had to chop open the ice every morning, and it would not stay open for long. Likewise, water had to be brought in for the fowls and the ducks. Food for the animals became a priority. Before the coming of the cold, Dad would chop up green corn stalks for ensilage, and store it in a silo trench. Eventually, a pit 12 feet wide and 20 deep was dug near the barn, and it was found that the ensilage kept better under such circumstances. When the winter was compounded by drought, a lot of water had to be mixed with the ensilage in the pit and thoroughly tramped down.

Food for the human inhabitants also required preservation for the winter. Out in front of the house we dug a hole and sunk an old washtub, for the storage of apples. To retrieve them, a snow shovel was required. In the rear of the house a cellar had been dug deep into the ground, and furnished with concrete shelves for the storage of fruit and vegetables: fruit in Agee jars, carrots in a big crock jar resting on sand, and potatoes on the floor .

Snow on the ground was the signal to butcher a surplus pig or two, and a steer. Bismarck, we know, claimed that one should not enquire too much about how laws and sausages are produced, but the latter is definitely an art, so I shall enlighten you. First you kill your pig. Unlike lambs, they don't go to the slaughter quietly; they fight and squeal, and by and large, let you know that they disapprove heartily of the whole procedure. Once the carcass has been gutted, it is placed on an old door or plank for phase two of the operation. A spadeful or two of ashes is added to boiling water, in order to produce caustic potash, which, when applied to the skin of the pig with a knife or scraper, makes removal of the hair easier. If the meat is hung on a tree overnight in cold weather, it is easier to cut up in the morning. You then slice up the pork and render down the fat in the boiler normally used for washing water. When this is pretty well completed, you get the men to put it through a special press to squeeze out the last drop of fat. At the bottom of the press was a heavy screen to hold the crackling, while the fat would drain out of a pipe at the bottom into a crock jar for storage and later use.

Some of the meat was canned in Agee jars, but Dad also had special recipes for curing hams in brine. Hams were hung in the cellar, as was the bacon – which was cured, along with the sausages, in the smoke-house out back. First of all, however, we had to clean out the intestines of the pig to use as casings for the sausages, while Dad used the stomach of the pig as a receptacle for blood pudding. Then metwurst was produced from ground up pork and beef, seasoned and smoked. We didn't waste much of that pig! In fact, what fat was not consumed as crackling, was turned into soap by Mum and Elda in the big copper kettle in the laundry shed.

In the kitchen itself, a wood stove served for cooking. Collecting the firewood was a full day's work, for in the fall of the year ie before the onset of winter made heating a priority, Dad and Uncle Ted would take several wagons down to the Blue River wagons. Attached to the sides of the wagon frames were bolsters to hold the wood. Having brought the firewood home, they would then connect the tractor to a belt and buzzsaw to reduce it to more manageable proportions. Anything which escaped this process was tackled with an axe. For good measure, corn cobs were also fed into the stove.

With the approach of winter, Dad would return from town with a wagonload of coal for the living room. The cast iron stove in that room was of a type known as a baseburner, where the coal had to be banked down for the night so that it would burn slowly, and not die. Therefore, in order for us to see whether it was burning properly, the door was furnished with a window constructed from isinglass, a transparent mica compound with a much higher melting point than true glass.

The laundry, or rather, wash house was a separate building, fifteen feet square. Here, the wooden tub was fitted with one of the modern cons: a washing machine connected by a belt to a Ronalson Tippet one cylinder engine. But, of course, there was no such thing as cold water washing in those days. The home-made pig-fat soap required hot water, and come the summer, when the winter's supply of firewood had been exhausted, dry cow pats, or manure, had to be collected from the fields as a substitute. That was one of my jobs. For those who are interested, cow pats smell a bit like burning grass but produce a good fire.

Next to the wash house stood the windmill (or, to be technically correct, the wind pump), which fed the underground water into a small steel frame tank, whose leaky interior had been cemented over. From there it ultimately flowed into the stock tank, to provide drinking water for the cows and horses. It also served us as a swimming pool when we returned, hot and dusty from a day's toil in the dry summer fields. But between the first tank and the stock tank lay another small tank, which served as a cool storage place for the cream. So successfully, in fact, did it serve this purpose, that one day Dad had a hired hand bring some ice cream back from town as a treat, and had it stored there. Alas! He forgot that ice cream, which is solid, requires a colder temperature than mere cream, which is a liquid. Instead of enjoying the treat, we found ourselves cleaning the melted ice cream out of the tank.

Youngsters are seldom idle on a farm. Every offspring is one extra unpaid contributor to the family economy. So, regularly as clockwork, morning and afternoon would see us up milking the cows by hand. Although Dad lacked the papers to prove it, they were purebred Holsteins from the state herd, and were excellent milk producers. Of course, once the milking was completed, the milk had to be fed into the hand-turned separator, to remove the cream. Dismantling, cleaning, and reassembling the machine after each separation was a tedious job which usually fell to Elda. In the meantime, the cream went off to market, to allow the purchase of necessities such as coffee, sugar, clothing, and occasionally food. As for the skimmed milk, the hogs grew fat on it, when it was fed to them with bran as a slop. Mum also used it to make cheese, and the buttermilk went into the pancakes we ate nearly every morning with fried eggs. (This was an American breakfast, remember, not an Australian one.) In fact, we grew or raised most of our own food, and Elda helped with the garden. We even had trees to provide our own apples, apricots, and mulberries. Ripe mulberries would be shaken from the tree onto a sheet underneath, to be turned into excellent pies and jams.

But I digress. Much later, when Ernest had already been ordained, I was about to join the seminary, and Lois to attend college, Dad realised that he was about to become short-handed for the twice daily milking ritual. He decided, therefore, to invest in a milking machine. Unfortunately, the cows had not been consulted, and they were not impressed. The summer before we left, we had to train them to adjust to metal, rather than human hands, and they did not accept it gracefully.

Indeed, if I may be permitted to get ahead of myself, once both of his sons were away, and before the milking machine was introduced, Dad brought in a young man from the orphanage in Muscatine, Iowa by name of Billy Seaman for what would now be called work experience. He and Mum then went off on holidays, leaving the farm in the hands of Billy and my cousin, Duane Philippi. These two worthies found it tiresome to have the cows flicking their tails at the flies while being milked by hand, because it meant they were also flicking the faces and shoulders of the milkers. They therefore cut off the tufts of hair on the ends of their tails. Of course, the result could have been predicted: they were now being swatted by the hard stumps of the tails instead of the hairs. In the meantime, the cows had to face the fields with their fly whisking apparatus seriously impaired, and their milk production suffered. When Dad came home, he was not amused.

But to get back on track: when a cow stall has been occupied all night, it is far from clean by sunrise. Every morning they had to be put out to water. In the really cold weather, they then had to come straight back in again, because frost bitten teats are definitely a hindrance to the milking process. But in the interval, short or long, when the stalls were unoccupied, yours truly was required to enter with a large shovel and heave the fresh manure out of a window two feet square. An obvious corollary was that, by the time of the spring thaw a large heap of ageing cow dung was standing outside the said window, rapidly turning odoriferous in the warmth. Not to worry: it was just the fertiliser required by the fields. Originally, we would haul it away in a spreader drawn by a team of Clydesdales or Percherons. Later, a John Deere tractor served the purpose. But there still remained the job of shoveling the stuff by hand into the spreader. Finally, we rigged up a scoop to the front of the tractor to alleviate that part of the work. Then Uncle Ted, from the next farm, with whom we shared the work, managed to attach a fork to the front of his tractor, and this served to collect both manure and hay.

You would be amazed to learn how such cattle stalls were constructed, so I shall relate an adventure which took place when I was about eight years old, at Uncle Will's place. A series of posts had been erected, and timber placed on top to support the roof. Over the posts was spread a lining of pig fencing wire, whose task was to hold the straw, because a roof made of straw was, believe it or not, more or less impervious to water. However, it had to be strong, because a layer of snow on top would greatly increase the weight. My father was driving the steam engine which ran the machine threshing the straw when suddenly, a spark from the steam engine caused the straw to burst into flames. There was no time to unhook the steam engine; Dad simply put it into gear and drove it out, while the other men seized the tongue of the threshing machine, with all the belts and pulleys still going strong, and steered it out of the way of the fire. Meanwhile, cousin Vic scaled the steeple of the barn in a frantic haste to wrap a wire screen around the cupola, lest the fire spread to the barn itself. Needless to say, that was the end of the threshing for some time.

Threshing was always a bit of a risk. The shocks of straw often served as a refuge for snakes. Not only were they a menace to the lads shifting the shock into the thresher, but sometimes a snake even got thrown into the thresher itself. After that, it was the turn of the man unloading the thresher to be careful. But for us children, the most important part of threshing was the end, when a big party was thrown in celebration.

Dad was a great one for horses. He loved them, and became an excellent amateur vet. If the local vet was too busy to attend the neighbour's animals, often they would call him to use his healing skills. (Contrary to popular belief, shooting is not the regular treatment for ailing horses.) The county also used our farm for demonstrations of horse hitches, with Dad as the chief demonstrator. Sometimes he would hook three together, sometimes five, one in front of the other. Dad even managed to develop an evener to hook two teams of horses together, so that neither had to pull more than its fair share of the load.

There wasn't a horse foaled that he couldn't handle, or any horse trick he couldn't see through. If a new horse had to be hitched to a wagon with an old, experienced breaking horse, a leather strap would be passed through a metal ring and around the newcomer's foreleg as a hobble. From the ring, a rope then led back to Dad's hand. After that, any misbehaviour on the part of the new horse would get it a tug on the hobble, and over the horse would go, onto its nose. One or two such spills was usually enough to teach it to be quiet.

Needless to say, I was the one who had to clean the manure out of the stables. I was also put on driving a team of three or five horses (Clydesdales or Percherons) on a mouldboard plough. Then I had to learn how to mow the hay with another team of horses, and rake it when it was dry. Dad would sow his oats and alfalfa by walking over a well tilled field with a hand held machine. The seed went into a canvas bag on top of a board, and a fan underneath would broadcast the seed as he cranked the handle. My job was to follow up with a team of horses and a harrow, spreading the soil back over the seed.

As I got older, I had to herd the milch cows back off the roadside, for during the drought they often wandered off the dry pastures, but on the highway they ran the risk of becoming road kill. To me, therefore, fell the task of bringing them back and providing them with fodder.

And sheep! In Nebraska the lambing season was freezing cold, but we had no choice but to go out and check on them, and when a ewe showed signs of reaching term, she would be transferred individually to a little pen four or five feet square. If the lamb failed to suckle, then it had to be introduced to a bottle. No-one with such a background has any difficulty with our Lord's account of the Good Shepherd.

> "The sheep hear his voice, and he calls his own sheep by name and leads them out. When he has brought out all of his own, he goes before them, and the sheep follow him, for they know his voice. A stranger they will not follow." (John 10: 3-5, RSV).

At night, when my call went out, they would come running, for they knew that some grain or hay was awaiting them. I used to count them as they passed through the gate. But when I returned from university, my call was in vain, for they no longer recognised my voice. People, in fact, are a lot like sheep – not least of all in their habit of following one another onto the wrong path. One sheep would find a hole in the fence, and the next thing, half the flock had wandered through, and it was up to the Good Shepherd to find them and bring them back.

Then there was the night Dad was brought out of bed by his cousin, Harry Hulse, the county sheriff, with three disreputable characters in tow. Apparently, their vehicle had broken down near Strang, and when the sheriff went out to offer assistance, he discovered a gunny sack full of live chickens. What rotten luck for the three desperados! But they had one source of hope: all chickens look alike, don't they?

"Well, Fred, can you identify these chickens?" he asked my father.

Would you believe? Dad had marked all his chickens with a punch hole in the right wing. The jig was up!

What with all these chores, someone is bound to ask:

didn't these farmer's kids ever get an education? Well, just across the road from our farm, on Highway Number 4 stood West Ward School: eight grades, one room, and a single teacher, named Alma Pape. From miles around trudged and rode every child of school age, in winter time lugging a contribution of coal for the indoor stove. At one point, some bright spark decided it would liven things up if he or she added a few .22 calibre rifle cartridges to the coal bucket – and yes, it did liven things up! More acceptable entertainment in the eyes of the adults was our rhythm band. While I strummed my ukulele, others beat away on triangles, spoons, a jew's harp, and even the rib bones of a steer – which is not an official musical instrument in most parts of the world, I agree. Come recess, we would charge outside for a game of softball. Then, at the end of the day, it was back home to milking the cows, fetching the sheep, shifting the cow manure, and following up our homework on reading, 'riting, and 'rithmetic.

It wasn't all bad. Hard work would be followed by homemade entertainment. Evening would see us gathered in the living room singing, and playing our individual musical instruments: Mum or Ernest on the piano, Dad with his violin, Ernest with a mouth organ, and I with a ukulele. In time, Lois also became proficient on the piano. On the Fourth of July, at the end of harvest, and other special occasions, out would come the homemade ice cream. The ice itself could be obtained from town, having been cut from a dam and stored throughout winter under a covering of hay or straw. Making the ice cream had always been great fun for us kids. It meant breaking off great chunks of ice, putting it in a burlap bag and smashing it with a stick. The ice was then packed around a circular metal churn, and ice added to make it freeze. Once the ice cream mixture was also added, it was churned by hand until the process was complete. Then we'd lick the churning paddle!

As the summer wore on, there was swimming in the nearby Blue River. But sometimes there was a surprise awaiting us. When the grasshoppers were swarming, we'd return to where we'd hung our clothes and find them eaten full of holes. Meanwhile, the men were fishing for catfish in the same river – Uncle Herman in particular. Once he even pulled a 20 pound fish out of a hole in the bank with his bare hands.

Another stretch of water about half a mile back on the farm held a special interest to us, for Dad had created it. He had used earthmoving equipment to dam up a natural hollow on the farm, and added an overflow pipe to maintain the water level, and prevent the dam from being washed away. Ducks found the pond a fatal attraction, for Dad had a hole dug in the central island to serve as a shooting blind. Access to the island was by means of a raft constructed by Dad from old telephone poles, which also gave us kids the opportunity to play Robinson Crusoe. With summer gone, winter would turn the pond into a natural skating rink. Then, when the snow set in in earnest, out would come our sleds, and we would slide down the slopes onto the dam.

Shooting was also a great pastime, for each of us had a BB gun or, as they are known in Australia, an air rifle. I can assure you, you need to be pretty effective with a firearm if you expect to hit something as small as a sparrow, but this we did on innumerable occasions. But when we were in earnest about getting rid of them, a simpler method was to venture out at night and pull them bodily from their nests. After the grain had been thrashed, the straw was thrown over a wire framework which provided a shelter for the livestock in winter, and it was here that the sparrows made their holes. Meanwhile, the pigeons would be roosting in the hay inside the barn, so we used to tackle them at night with torches and our BB guns. At least pigeons provided some good eating – which is more than can be said for sparrows.

But guns, let me tell you, are not something you should play around with. At this point I should explain that I had two cousins, Louis and Billy, born within two months of me. When the three of us were together, anything could happen, and usually did. The result was one of my father's favourite sayings :

"One kid is just a kid; two kids are half a kid, and three kids are no kid at all" ie they could not be controlled or reasoned with. Indeed, we were known as the Katzenjammer Kids after those terrible brothers in the popular comics. (Look it up on the internet if you're too young to remember.)

Anyway, Louis had constructed a makeshift pistol by sawing off most of the barrel of an old rifle. Then, one night, when the families were together, we Katzenjammer Kids got hold of some old .22 calibre cartridges, and decided it would be a great idea to place them one by one on an old brick, belt them with a hammer, and make them explode towards the corncrib. If the adults had had any sense, they would have put a stop to it at the first sound of an explosion, but out on the farm you get cavalier about explosions. Then, somebody decided we could make an even better bang if we could fire them in the pistol, without shooting the lead out. We therefore broke off the lead of the cartridge by shoving it into the end of the barrel first. It was great fun, and the pistol was passed from hand to hand until it came to mine. What I didn't know was that, this time, the lead had not been ejected from the barrel on the last exercise. With the bravado and carelessness of boyhood, I leveled the pistol in the direction of the car where the girls were sitting. There was a loud explosion, followed by a shattering of glass and a scream. The window was broken, and Louis' sister, Orlene was bleeding from the forehead. Absolute panic and pandemonium ensued. For a minute we thought she was dead. Then our parents rushed her to the doctor, and she was all right. As for the pistol, Louis threw it into the outside toilet.

As for the women, they preferred to occupy themselves with milder pursuits. Croquet was a major summer activity. At the end of harvest, a feast of pies and cakes would be brought out for the family and the harvest crew. Then the winter settled in, when work at least slackened off, and home entertainment came into its own. Groups of friends would gathered at somebody's place, get out the cards, and play cribbage, pitch, pinochle, rummy, and a gambling game called solo. Only the men played that, but instead of poker chips, they used kernels of corn. A gambling game, you must understand, is not much fun unless you actually have stakes to win or lose, but our crowd had philosophical objections to gambling with money. (Also, of course, they didn't have any money.) Dad also had a broad repertoire of cards tricks for the amusement of strangers, and, you may be interested to learn, Lois can still perform some of them.

Of course, in any close knit community – even a small one – there is always a large and regular cycle of birthdays and anniversaries. A group known locally as the Knutson Gang appointed themselves as the chief custodians and organisers of celebrations for these occasions. We children would play, the women would chat, and the men would play cards. But at the end of the night we would all gather round the piano and sing and sing and sing. And always, the last song of the night would be, "God Be With You Till We Meet Again." It became the theme song of my life, to be sung with special poignancy at every parting, for often we had no idea when we would meet again, if at all.

Ah, the idyllic life of a country boyhood! Don't you believe it! Here's a couple of terms you may have forgotten: Great Depression, and Dust Bowl. On October 29, 1929, when I had been in the world less than three years, too young to know the meaning of normality and prosperity, the stock market crashed – and nowhere did it crash heavier than in the United States itself. Overnight, businesses closed down and soup kitchens opened up. In the following three years, stock prices fell 80 per cent. People's life savings vanished into thin air as 5,000 banks went belly up, and unemployment soared to 25 per cent. Honest workmen were turned into hoboes, drifting down the highways and railways, cadging for food and work.

Meanwhile, out on the land, farm prices had been low even during the 1920s. Now there was no-one to buy our produce. Soon there was no produce to sell. On the heels of the Depression came a drought of truly biblical proportions: seven lean years without an intervening fat year. The apple and apricot trees shriveled up and died. The wheat crop, on which the family relied for its flour, failed. One year, when walking through town, Dad happened to run into Rudy Collison, the local miller, who raised the issue about how he hadn't been to see him. "Well, the fact is," Dad told him, "we have no wheat to grind. All we got back from this year's harvest was enough seed for next year's crop."

Mr Collison, bless him! was sympathetic. "Take what flour you need," he told him, "and pay me back when your crop comes in." From that day on at least, we were given our daily bread.

And the dust! Nebraska is on the edge of the Dust Belt. When the horizon turned dark with dust, school was canceled for the day, and we all scattered, each to his or her own farm. In the van of the wind swept the tumbleweeds, two or three feet in diameter, rolling along until they met a wire fence, where they clustered and piled up. Then the dust piled up into the tumbleweeds, turning the fence into a solid wall, built of the topsoil of men's dreams.

Our crop of alfalfa withered and died, and the ground collapsed under it. No longer were the roots of the plants – which went down as much as twenty feet, searching for water – able to hold the soil together. Great holes appeared in the field, to be appropriated by wandering skunks and civet cats. With the approach of bad weather, the stinking cats sought shelter in our workshop – much to the consternation of its human occupants.

Bitter were those years. A pan of whole wheat would be left soaking in water overnight, and Mum would cook it for breakfast. Sometimes we had corn mush or oatmeal, and a major component of our diet was cornbread and homemade sauerkraut. The cabbage, or "Kraut", we grew in our own garden. While one of us sat in a chair holding the kraut cutter, another would feed the head through until it was fully shredded, after which it was packed into a crock jar about two feet high and a foot an a half wide, and pressed down with salt. A brick on top of a plate served as a lid, and once the Kraut was sufficiently "saur", it was canned in the all purpose Agee jars and set aside for winter.

The resurrection box was the label given by Mum to a cardboard container into which went any old clothes provided by friends and relatives. At her leisure – and there wasn't much of that! – she would unpick them, and convert them into "new" garments for the family. By this time, Ernest, by now aged about 17, had finished high school, and was attending a two year course at Hebron, preparatory to entering the ministry. So desperate were our finances that Mum actually bleached the inscriptions off some old flour bags and turned them into sets of underpants for him. He claimed they were surprisingly soft.

Over the gravel and dirt thoroughfares, the ten mile drive to Hebron was still a major undertaking, but least by now our horse-drawn buggy had been replaced by a Model T Ford. But you mustn't fancy that this concession to mechanised progress was in any way comparable to its Twenty-first Century counterparts. For a start, it didn't start unless the crankshaft was inserted into the front and physically twisted by hand, and if the spark lever were in the wrong position, it was likely to backfire, and threaten to break the arm of the person doing the cranking. And who would that person be? Well, with Dad behind the wheel, and Ernie in the passenger seat, that left only one other male in the family, if you get my drift. To make it even more fun, in winter time the engine tended not to start unless you first jacked up the back wheel, to relieve the pressure on the oil, which had congealed with the cold. Thank goodness it only had to be done on Mondays, for he boarded at college during the week! Luckily, cousin Vic Bruning would sometimes provide a lift, whenever he was headed for nearby Byron, to pay court to the girl he eventually married.

In 1940 the crunch came. Dad had a mortgage of $4,000

on the farm, held by Uncle Reuben, my mother's brother, and his wife, Aunt Gerty. $4,000 was an awful lot of money in 1940, especially when a drought has left you penniless, and the debt was foreclosed. His heart was heavy as he and Mum went into Bruning to sign over the farm to Uncle Reuben. Then, as he was fond of telling in later life, he said to Mum, "Well, I still have a few cents in my pocket, so there's no point in being sad. Let's head for the soda fountain and have an ice cream each."

Reuben and Gerty later sold the farm and used the proceeds to become alcoholics, and my parents ended up taking care of them. A subtle change now took place in Dad. The old farm had been the centre of his life, but now it was gone, in its place came a realisation of the transitoriness of earthly ventures. The farm was no longer first anymore; instead there was a *faith* which took him through to his death at nearly 97. I, too, learned a lesson: that there is no point in holding bitterness or a desire for revenge in your heart. You can safely leave it to the Lord to deal with such matters.

In the meantime, here was I at age 13, and the only home, and the only financial support, I had known had been pulled out from under me. The only fallback position was the old Philippi homestead, where Grandpa and Grandma used to live before they moved into Bruning. Dad's brother, Ted had taken it over, but now he had just lost his first wife, Olga, and had moved to Bruning to take over the gas station (petrol station to you Australians) there. That left our family to occupy the farm. Fortunately, droughts do not last for ever, and bit by bit, during the 1940s, the good times returned. Eventually, Dad found it possible to buy out the rest of his family. Once more, he had a farm.

Those years were still hard. Horses used to cost a fortune to feed over winter, so finally he decided to sell them and purchase a tractor. Tractors are by no means cheap, but at least you don't have to pour a gallon of petrol into their tanks every day they stand idle. His first one was an old Fordson, but it was so heavy Dad used to aver that every time a cow pissed the old girl would get stuck. He therefore replaced it with a John Deere one cylinder tractor, which ran on kerosene once you had primed it with petrol, which you did by turning the flywheel by hand. Originally, the wheels were of steel, set with large vertical lugs for traction, but that made it difficult to manage (not to mention uncomfortable!), so Dad cut them off and welded on rims for tyres. Even they were subject to slippages, so he filled the tyres with water, topped off with some sort of antifreeze in winter. As I said, the modern generation wouldn't have a clue about what went on in the olden days. But at least he got the tractor paid off fairly quickly, followed by the farm itself.

By now, Lois was old enough to accompany me to school – the big teenager on a full grown mare called Daisy, the little girl on Toy, the Shetland pony. After a ride of three mile [five kilometres], we would leave them at Granddad Philippi's farm for the day and then proceed another mile on foot to school. These were no ordinary horses. Toy, who had been acquired from Uncle Ted, had originally belonged to a circus, and had a few tricks of his own. He had a habit of rolling over when you least expected it, or else he would take off into a swamp ditch and rub your leg against a stump in order to remove you from his back – habits not exactly endearing to a six year old girl. As for Daisy, we knew she was expecting, but didn't know exactly when. One bitter winter day, with snow on the ground, we came back from school to find a brand new foal next to Daisy. I immediately got on the phone to Dad.
"Well," he said, "I suppose I'd better come down with the car and trailer and bring the horse back. Lois can come back with me, and you can ride Toy home."
From then on, he would take us to school by car whenever it got too cold to expect the horses to go outdoors. (I said horses, not children.)
As children, naturally, we had been on the back of ponies

as soon as we were old enough to ride. Some time later, Dad decided it was time I got a new horse to ride, and took me to Geneva to purchase one. "I don't know," he said, as we checked one out. "It looks like it might be doped." But when I rode it, everything seemed fine, so we bought it. Lois was also delighted, because it meant she could graduate from Toy to Daisy. But the next morning, it was a different story. No sooner was I on its back, when it flew into a frenzy of bucking. As I picked myself off the ground, blood streaming from my mouth and nose, Dad seized the bridle and brought it under control. The next thing, the horse had been dragged back to its original owner. Dad got his money back, and the other guy got a large piece of Dad's mind.

Once more there were cattle and sheep, and pigs. And chickens – 600 of them. This time, our parents had a contract with the local hatchery, which provided them with roosters for breeding. Agents of the hatchery would also come down and prick each of the birds under the wing to obtain a blood sample, and if the fowl wasn't up to scratch, it was sold. That way, we were assured of a better price for our eggs. In this predecessor of a battery henhouse, the floor was of wire mesh to prevent the droppings accumulating where the eggs could roll into it. A couple of times a month the fowl manure had to be cleaned out. You will have noticed by now that much of the work around a farm consists of cleaning up after animals. But the manure made great fertiliser.

During those years I also went hunting with Dad. I was now big enough to hold and use a single barrel, 12 gauge shotgun, and later on he bought me a repeater Winchester 12 gauge shotgun, and we would go hunting pheasants and rabbits together. The pheasants, of course, made good eating for the humans, and the rabbits went to the dogs. But the incident that really rattled me was the time the men of the district decided to clear a seven square mile [18 square kilometres] patch in the Red Cloud district of rabbits and coyotes one cold, snow-clad winter's day. Forming a cordon around the area, we all simultaneously headed into the centre, and any coyote or rabbit flushed out in front of our guns was history. As the perimeter shrank, the hunters naturally dropped out one by one to avoid danger from the shooters remaining. At the end of the day, one truck was piled high with rabbit carcasses, next to a smaller pile of dead coyotes.

We had all been trained in the handling of guns, and knew to ensure they were not loaded when no longer in use. A firearm must always be treated like a poisonous snake, ready to strike unexpectedly if not kept at a safe distance. But a certain cousin, who shall remain nameless, was known to be a bit careless in that regard. Here we were, about to head home, when I threw my foot onto the running board of the truck. Suddenly, there was a loud explosion, as his shotgun went off, blasting a fan of 12 gauge pellets just where my foot had been. When my heart stopped pounding, I thanked God for His protection, because I could easily have ended up crippled.

While on the new farm, I passed two milestones. Having completed eight years of primary school, I finished my four years of high school. The demands of farm work provided little leisure time for sports, but I did enjoy performing in one-act plays, and we received several awards.

Also, I got confirmed. Our parents' strong Christian faith had been the ever-present background of our lives. Dad always credited our mother for bringing it into the family. When they were married, she had told them they would have to begin their married life with daily devotions, and so it was. Thus, when Sunday came around, we never questioned attending church and Sunday school. Confirmation classes under Pastor Cronek took up two years of Saturday mornings as well. We were required to memorise the whole catechism, and a large number of hymns. But what the pastor really imparted was a faith, and a sense of God's grace, which has stayed with me ever since.

1944 came and went, and with it the last of my school days. Somehow I had to decide what to do with my life. Ernie was going into the ministry. As the only son left behind, I was naturally expected to follow my father on the farm. Farming, of course, was in his blood; he could not imagine any other life. But I could not get out of my mind the drought, the dust, the debt, the unremitting toil and precarious rewards. I didn't know what I wanted to be, but one thing I knew I did *not* want to be was a farmer. However, I had an older brother as an example. I would become a pastor.

In the summer of 1944 I went to Capital University in Columbus, Ohio as a pre-seminary student. My family paid what they could and I also had to work while at school. I served in a bakery and a big supermarket, and obtained a chauffeur's licence so that I could drive the rich people of Bexley around. I also managed to purchase a bicycle for $5, and when I left school, I was able to sell it for $10. Ernie was already there. In fact, the following year he asked me to be his best man when he married Ann Helwick. But as far as my own studies went, things were getting unstuck. What I had forgotten was that the ministry is not a career; it is a calling. If God has not called you, you will go nowhere. I had seen it essentially as an alternative to farming; my heart was not in it. Just the same, in hindsight, I can see how even this fitted into God's plan, for it began a series of events which would change, not only my life, but also those of others around me. My grades were sinking, and so was my heart when I was summoned to the Dean's office. I had failed, flunked, shot my bolt. My plans were in ruins. But my presence there was not a total waste, and he sent me over to consult Dr Beuhering at the seminary. It was he who put the proposition to me: would I be prepared to go to New Guinea?

Chapter 2
New Guinea Beckons

New Guinea? New Guinea? What's with New Guinea? International geography is not traditionally a strong point among Americans, but I couldn't plead complete ignorance. I'd read about it in missionary magazines, and anybody who followed the progress of the Pacific War would know that it was the large island just north of Australia. But it had not loomed large on my horizon until now.

Stretched out east to west, just south of the Equator, culturally and ethnically a part of Melanesia, it resembled nothing so much as a bird, with the northeastern tip appropriately labeled Vogelkop, or bird's head, and the tail extending out into the southwest. A vertical line down the centre of the map separated the western Dutch half from the eastern section under Australian control. Originally, in the previous century, Germany had annexed the northeastern part, and Queensland, in a fit of alarm, persuaded the British Government to annex the southeastern section, known as Papua. When Queensland joined the Commonwealth of Australia at federation, the administration of Papua was transferred to Australia. At the outbreak of the First World War, Australia marched in and conquered German New Guinea. This left the Lutheran missions, strung out along the northeast coast, out on a limb. During the interwar period, the German staff were largely replaced by Lutheran missionaries from the United States. And now these missions were in a state of total devastation from the effects of the Second World War. They needed volunteers to repair the damage – volunteers skilled in carpentry and handyman work. And if there is one thing life on a farm teaches you, it is carpentry and handyman skills. Indeed, sixty years later, they are still my passion and my hobby.

You can easily imagine my mixed emotions of surprise,

relief, excitement, and trepidation. But the issue was really never in doubt. When God slams one gate shut in your face, and immediately throws open another next to it, it is pretty obvious which path you are expected to take. In the meantime, however, it was winter, and I was a thousand miles from home, and broke. I decided to do something I would not recommend today: Ihit the highway, using my thumb as a ticket. At this distance in time, I cannot, for the life of me, remember what I used for accommodation on the way, but I do remember that my last lift was with an off-duty policeman, who delivered me right to my surprised parents' front door.

Now came the task of gaining their consent – required not only by common courtesy and the Ten Commandments, but also the law, because the age of majority in those days was twenty-one, and I was only nineteen. Initially, their reaction was dumbfounded amazement, then consternation. You want to go *where*? And for two and a half years? What sort of terrible, God-forsaken place is that? And at your age? But, of course, boys of my age had already gone to the same area for the same length of time, and as combat soldiers, not peaceful volunteers. At least they shouldn't expect me to be shot at.

The church would contribute $150 to pay for the special clothes and equipment needed in the tropics (including pith helmets!), as well as all our expenses from leaving home to our return. We also received some literature on the country, so we wouldn't be completely in the dark when we arrived. Also, we would be paid $150 a year for incidentals. I know that sounds like chicken feed now, but at the time it was quite reasonable – especially since it was basically pocket money.

The process initially moved with the usual glacial speed. The official notification was effective from April 3, 1946, and my first passport was issued on August 1st. Oh, yes, and the church authorities advised my family that, what with the slowness of the mail in that part of the world, they may not hear from me for six to twelve months. They were quite dismayed. According to Lois – I myself have forgotten it - on the day of my departure, they were all weeping, while I sat in the next room, accompanying myself on the piano singing, "Bless This House".

So it was, in late September, that I found myself in San Francisco in the company of six other Americans and two Canadians, ranging in age from 17 to a hoary 28, ready for the great adventure. (Later, when we were already in New Guinea, a volunteer from Australia would make up a tenth.) For the first time in my life, I came face to face with the sea: one vast, watery prairie a hundred times as broad as any prairie I'd ever encountered, and the thought that we were about to embark on it for the other side of the world was awe inspiring. The addition of missionaries, nurses, and assorted staff brought our group to thirty-three. The congregation of the Lutheran Church of the Good Shepherd held a dinner in our honour, and for the first time in my life I tasted venison.

My Australian visa (valid for only six months!) was not received until September 26, two days before we were set to depart. Our home for the next nineteen days would be the S.S. *Monterey*, an ocean liner turned troopship, now returning to civilian duties for the first time with a manifest of 900 passengers. My chief memory of that voyage was the bunks: eight crammed into a cabin originally designed for four, the bottom of each a short, skull-smashing gap from the one below. But it was still an ocean liner. The meals were good, and there were movies and dancing, not to mention chapel, and we got to call in at Samoa, Fiji, and New Zealand. It wasn't too bad, provided you didn't want to sit upright in bed, or swing a cat.

At 11 a.m. on 17 October we docked in Sydney Harbour, only to discover – would you believe? - it was in the middle of a dock strike. For Australians such circumstances were, and would be for many years to come, accepted as a normal part of life, but it was somewhat disconcerting for us newcomers to find our luggage just sitting unattended on the wharf, for us to sort through and have inspected by Customs, a process which lasted hours on end. We had been met at the wharf by our

Australian contact, the Rev Christoph Stolz and his wife, Regina, but it was not until 9 at night that they were able to introduce us to our accommodation: a quite basic Salvation Army hotel entitled the People's Palace. Even then, the long day was not over. The Stolzes' church provided us with a welcome dinner at half past 10. And so to bed! Our mattresses were padded with cornhusks, and slip slided away with every toss and turn.

The next day, Rev Stolz assisted us in changing our currency, and getting our paperwork started. (For a start, my six month visa definitely needed to be extended.) Not all of our thirty-three could leave at once; instead transportation would be arranged on the basis of personal importance: women and children first, and volunteer builders last of all.

Forty years after the events, Esther Dockter Wegenast, the wife of one of the volunteers, chronicled our adventures in a book, of which I ensured every member of my family received a copy. So I might as well quote her account of one of my own experiences[1]:

> Some days later when the mission builders took a meal at a restaurant, Philippi requested a napkin – one of those table items American use.
>
> "A napkin?" the waitress returned, looking around at all the fellows, studying them. "You are sure you want a napkin?"
>
> "Sure," Philippi assured her, a knowing smile on his face.
>
> "Right. A napkin it will be." The waitress left.
>
> The fellows smiled. Self-assuranced *[sic]*. Their waitress returned, bearing a large square of white terry cloth. "Here you are," she said casually and left again.
>
> The fellows stared a the large cloth big enough for a diaper. "This is a napkin?" they all said.   "You did say

---

[1] Esther Dockter Wegenast (1996), *In His Service*, limited edition of 300, self-published. 94 pp, at p21

'napkin' didn't you, Philippi?" the fellows asked. "Ask her again."

When the waitress returned, Philippi explained to her that he wanted a napkin.

"This is a napkin, sir ... a baby's napkin..."

"But I want something to clean my hands ..."

"Oh, what you want is a serviette! What you asked for was a baby's ... diaper. Sorry about that."

Golly! And I thought they spoke English over there!

Now the waiting began – waiting for our paperwork to be actioned, waiting for the strike to end, waiting for transport to arrive, waiting for the more important members to leave. We couldn't even go back to get our trunks off the wharf; they had to remain there either because of the strike, or because they were waiting for shipment. All we had to live out of was our on-board luggage. Fortunately, Sydney had its attractions. It was no New York, but it was at least the largest city in Australia, and we were small town country boys. Also, Rev Stolz's congregation – bless them! - frequently put on entertainment. But time dragged. It was with tremendous relief when we got passage on board the S.S. *Duntroon* – after twenty-six days!

A greater difference from the *Monterey* could scarcely be imagined. We were aboard an inter-island trader with limited, albeit surprisingly comfortable accommodation for passengers. For a start, we could sit upright in our bunks for a change. It took five and a half days of leisurely sailing the coast of Queensland before we arrived at Port Moresby, the hot, dry capital of Australian New Guinea. Here was our first taste of the strange new world we were entering, as we hiked a couple of miles to a native village, where the people sang for us, and then asked us to pay. Three days later, we reached our destination, Lae.

Culture shock hit us with a vengeance! Not even Port Moresby had prepared us for the green luxuriance and the steamy heat of the north of the island. Midsummer in Nebraska could get as hot as this, but out on the farm, you merely scorched, you did not swelter, and the temperature always dropped at night. Down here, you'd be lucky if the night time temperature fell below 80° F – which was also pretty much the percentage humidity. It was now 21 November. Back home they would be banking down the fire at night, and awakening in the morning to snow on the ground. Here there was neither summer nor winter, just two seasons: hot and wet, and hot and very wet.

Two miles down the road, at the prewar mission station of Ampo, we were introduced to the temporary mission headquarters. It was just an old army warehouse, with a dirt floor and walls of sheet iron up to chest height, and then arc mesh – the sort used for reinforcing concrete - up to the corrugated iron roof – enough to allow at least some ventilation while the tropical sun converted the iron roof and walls into an oven. That was all very well, but what about our living quarters? They were here – behind the makeshift furniture of mission HQ, at the rear of the warehouse: there stood our bunks, complete with netting to keep out the mosquitoes – not to mention any slightest breath of cooling breeze once the sun set.

Let me quote Mrs Wegenast again[2]:

> A place run over with myriads of ants, centipedes, millipedes, scorpions, termites, mosquitoes, cockroaches, spiders, lizards, and snakes – all household words – was no place for a finicky housewife or anyone terrified of the likes. Ants, found in food, clothing, bed sheets, wall, floor, ceilings – in the sugar bowl – seemed clearly in control. Cockroaches and termites could be heard chewing on paper and wood at nigh, but one had better get used to them. Deliberately allowing geckos (small, transparent lizards) to crawl around on the ceiling and walls of a house as a way of controlling bugs came as a surprise to any first-timer.

[2] Wegenast, *op. cit.* p 28

Centipedes, millipedes and scorpions lurking in damp, dark places, particularly damp clothes, were warned against. Also death adders. Pythons, huge, sluggish, but harmless to a point, posed no immediate danger. "Check your bed sheets at night before crawling into bed," was the immediate advice given to the builders, "and shake out your shoes in the morning before slipping into them. Many a person has stepped into a pair of shoes and was rewarded with a squish or something very painful, perhaps a snake, a centipede, a scorpion, or a tarantula."

And the mosquitoes! They were more than a nuisance; they were an absolute menace. Malaria was endemic throughout the entire island. In fact, in later years, in the Ramu Valley, I would discover villages almost completely bereft of old people. They had all died prematurely of malaria. As a result, we spent the whole two and a half years with faces turned yellow from the Atebrin taken as a prophylaxis. It produced interesting comments from our families when we returned home! Even so, we all suffered bouts of malaria several times, and had to be treated with high doses of quinine.. Later, when I suffered a relapse back in America, I had to provide the diagnosis for my doctor, because he had never encountered it before. The malarial parasite has the nasty habit of lurking in your liver at one stage of its life cycle, whence it ventures into the blood stream to cause fever and shakes. Since the liver is the detoxifying organ of the body, it tends to denature any medicine sent to cure it. It was only much later, when medical science came up with a new drug, Primaquine that I was at last freed from these relapses.

I do not wish, however, to overstate the negative aspects of our stay. We were young, and this was an adventure. We were enthusiastic, and threw ourselves into the task with a gusto that our native helpers, with perhaps a more realistic view of work in an enervating tropical environment, did not appreciate. When we tried to get them to work as hard as us, they went on strike!

The workers themselves – the native Melanesians – bore only a superficial resemblance to our American Negroes. They had black skin and flat noses, but their hair was frizzy rather than curly, and they lacked the thick lips, high foreheads, and fine bone structure of the children of Africa. They were an ancient race, related to the Aborigines of Australia. Back in the hinterland, their traditional lifestyle was that of Stone Age horticulturists, counting their wealth in pigs, wearing skirts and loincloths of grass or bark, and making war on, and occasionally eating, the inhabitants of the next valley or mountain who, as likely as not, spoke a different language. At least 700 languages served a population of only 1.4 million.

Ironically, this very fragmentation had its own advantages. It is one of the reasons that, since independence, Papua New Guinea has avoided the *coups d'état* which have plagued Africa. No "tribe" is bog enough to provide a large enough support base for an ambitious general or would-be dictator. At the same time, it meant that Australia could dominate the country without colonial wars or, indeed, even an army. A police force, largely composed of the natives themselves, was sufficient.

We had found ourselves in a political system foreign to the outlook of most Americans. An independent branch of the British Empire was carving out a second generation empire of its own – and largely under the radar of its own citizens. Australian rule was peaceful, paternalistic, and benevolent. Not much lip service was given to racial equality, but a lot to The White Man's Burden. Scattered along the coasts, and throughout the highlands and valleys, dwelt approximately 10,000 white people: traders, planters, miners, teachers, missionaries, and, at the apex, a small group of administrators valiantly seeking to bring health, wealth, education, and law and order to a land where witchcraft, warfare, cannibalism, headhunting, and debilitating tropical diseases had held sway for thousands of   years.

Anyhow, here we were, and were immediately set to work building a permanent mission headquarters and guest house.

Within a very short time we discovered that the pith helmets we had brought along were vastly inferior to the Australian slouch hat, and even a shirt felt superfluous. It is a wonder that I haven't suffered more in later life from skin cancers. The days would see us shirtless and tanned under the steamy tropical sun, and when the rain struck, as it did every day, we as often as not worked through it. It was a choice of being either soaked with rain or soaked with sweat, and at least the rain was slightly cooler. In the meantime, Art Fenske, our chief scrub clearer, discovered live hand grenades adhering to the tracks of his bulldozer. Fortunately, the pins had been rusted tight. Not so fortunate had been the owner of the skeleton he also uncovered among the vegetation, and whose identity remains a mystery to this day.

Of course, it soon became obvious that, in order to get anything done, we had to quickly master the local vehicular language, Pidgin, which had been introduced to Melanesia even before the Germans arrived. What can I say about Pidgin? Initially, it looks like broken English, but a deeper investigation will reveal a smattering of loan words from German, Portuguese, and distant Melanesian languages, along with a grammar all of its own.

Let us take the sentence: *Bikpela pik i-bagarap-im ol gaden bilong yumi*. This represents a Melanesian attempt to say: "Big-fellow pig he bugger up him all garden belong you-me", and can be translated: "A/the big pig is ruining/has ruined our gardens." There stand the key features of Pidgin in a nutshell:

- No articles.
- No plurals. Use *ol*.
- No tenses. Time is not stipulated in every single verb, as in English, but by the context, or by a judicial sprinkling of adverbs, such as *pinis* (finish), *baimbai* (by 'n' by), or *stap* (stop). This last meant, initially, to stop still, then to stay, to continue in one place, and finally to continue an activity – which, of course, is the exact opposite of the meaning of

"stop" in English.

- All verbs with a noun subject start with *i-*.
- All transitive verbs end in *-im*.
- The possessive, or "of", is represented by *bilong*. For nearly every other preposition use *long*.
- The English speakers who first brought broken English to the Pacific islands believed that a foreigner will understand the language if it is not only simplified, but also rendered ungrammatical. Hence the quite unnecessary addition of the suffix, *-pela* to nearly every adjective.
- Likewise, not being the most refined or polite members of Anglophone society, they believed that slang, or even vulgar expressions were more easily understood that everyday ones. The verb in the above sentence is only one example.
- Finally, although Pidgin lacks the fine shades of meaning possible in English, there is one area in which it is more specific. When the words, "we", "us" or "our" are used in English, only the context tells you whether the person spoken to is included. No such ambiguity is present in Pidgin. In the above sentence, *yumi* indicates that it was your garden as well as mine which was damaged. If they belonged to my neighbour and me, but not you, I would have to say *mipela*. If you were also included along with my neighbour and me, another term would apply. The variations are endless.

On   4 January 1946, I was one of four posted to Malolo, a hill station about five miles from Salamaua. Our job was to rebuild the bombed out roadway, and put in a new water pump and pipeline. It meant inserting an hydraulic ram into a spring, then raising the water 165 feet vertically and about 1000 feet horizontally to the mission station, using some of the water to power the pump itself. In our spare time, we did a lot of swimming. But this was quite different from the swimming hole on the farm. At one point, what with the tide and the undercurrent, I found myself too far from shore for my

Nebraska bred swimming skills to cope. Fearing for my life, I nevertheless found a log to cling to while I extended my strength to return to shore.

On 23 January 1947 we sailed on the S.S. *Umboi* to Finschhafen. What a surprise! Here was a six lane highway made of white coral, huge trucks with six wheel drives for us to use, plus jeeps, weapon carriers, and the like. One of the largest military bases in the Pacific was being dismantled – in a fashion impossible to justify if the home population had been informed. Hundreds, probably thousands of tons of usable equipment were being deliberately destroyed. Binoculars and toilets were being smashed less somebody actually find a use for them. While the climate was turning our own boots mouldy, mountains of surplus shoes were being burned or treated with corrosive chemicals. Larger items were being buried or thrown into the sea. At the same time, other items were just left lying around for any enterprising scavenger to collect. We managed to rescue a number of rifles in this fashion, and were able to go on the occasional hunt. I still have a photo of a cassowary shot in this fashion.

Not to be left behind were the American war dead. A team of Filipino scouts was busy with the loathsome job of digging up 10,000 bodies from the local cemetery for shipment back to the States. They were welcome to the job, but some of our crew had to help shift the coffins because the bridge was out over the Mape River, and the army had no transport.

Apart from hunting, our spare time allowed us swimming in the local stream, as well as at Scarlet Beach, the scene of some bloody combat during the war. We also formed a singing quarter around the piano while our supervisor's wife, Lydia Yetmar, played. I still treasure one of the red hymnbooks which I acquired at that time, which the army had left behind.

Initially, we were set to miscellaneous construction work. We helped put in the 10 cm cast iron water line to provide the hospital with a good water supply. Then Russell Scherer, an engineer from Ohio, came and added a Pelton wheel to the stream to provide us with electricity, but it had its limitations. If too many lights or appliances were used, the voltage would drop, and everything would go dim.

The hospital also required two toilets for its native patients, and we were asked to construct them overhanging the sea, so that the tide could flush out the waste. And thereby hangs a tale. I was inside, working with a planer, when Harry Vorrath suddenly noticed a shark cruising nearby. With a shout of "Sharks!", he rushed up to the hospital to collect his .303 rifle. Exactly why he thought the shark deserved a .303 shell is now lost in the mists of time, but his actions provide another classic example of why guns should be treated with care. As he was running back to the site of the latrine, the rifle went off. The bullet ricocheted around inside the latrine, hit the planer, and shattered. I felt a sharp pain, and stumbled out, blood streaming from my leg, and announced that I had been shot. Fortunately, they proved to be only very minor, superficial wounds.

In March our real Finschhafen assignment began: the warehouses. Forty-eight of them lay scattered higgledy-piggledy over the countryside, ranging in length from 100 feet to a record 690 feet. The Lutheran church had recognized them as a good source of lumber for its hospital and mission complex in Madang, and had purchased it from the departing military at a fire sale price. Our job was to pull 'em down, slice 'em up, and ship 'em out. Better get cracking! Two or three of us, with the help of eight to ten native staff, would tackle one each day. In a short time, a system had been developed: get the native staff to remove the galvanized iron roofing, chop and saw through the first truss section, pull down that section with a rope, the move on to the other section. At one point, however, it nearly ended disastrously. I was working inside while Clarence Wegenast started cutting through some braces. Suddenly, it became apparent that, in this particular warehouse, the posts were not anchored in concrete, and the whole structure was about to collapse. There was nothing to do but run for our lives. The two native "boys" on the roof were in a perilous position, but one of them suffered nothing more than injuries to his heels, while the other one – believe it or not! - safely rode the iron sheet down like a surfboard.

Leon Philippi, master builder

Once a warehouse was demolished, the work was not finished. First, the timber had to be cut into manageable pieces. Not only that but, also acquired with one of the warehouses, were a thousand tons of cement in 100 pound sacks. About two thirds of them were Australian, and were useless, the cement having congealed with the tropical moisture. But the American ones, protected by an extra layer of covering, were salvageable, and it fell to us to sort them out and, with the help of the native staff, move them to the dock. When we weren't busy on that, there was always the task of searching the bush for drums of petrol, and hauling firewood.

When the M.V. *Malaita* arrived, it took three days to load it. But there still remained the problem of the church's heavy equipment: a grader, two bulldozers, an earth-moving machine, an army six wheel drive, a weapons carrier – which could serve as a substitute Land Rover - cement mixers, forklifts, jeeps, trucks, and a compact repair shop on wheels. Fortunately, this was where we were able to call in a favour; because of our former assistance in moving the American war dead, the army had provided us with an L.S.T. (Landing Ship, Tank). On 5 September 1947, the *Malaita* departed for Madang, arriving twelve hours later, some time after the L.S.T.

After a few days of unloading, we got started constructing a workshop and store. The crew was very proud of the beautiful job we did hand-trowelling down the concrete slab for the store, but in the morning we discovered it peppered with neat circular holes the size of a two shilling piece. It was totally bewildering, until closer inspection revealed the skins of peas in some of them. Then the penny dropped. Some dried peas had spilt in the ship's hold, along with a bag of cement. When the cement was repacked, some of the peas must have been inadvertently included. The addition of moisture during the night, as well as heat from the cement curing, had caused them to pop.

A host of additional tasks now demanded our attention: rebuilding the mission wharf, constructing a home for the pastor, helping with the printery, and wiring the machine house at Nagada, to name just a few. Certain incidents stick in my memory. For instance, while we were building the workshop, we had to work around the casket of a nurse, Marie Kroeger, who had died while a prisoner of the Japanese. At one point, a ship, the *Mintoro* brought in a herd of half-wild cattle to restock the plantation, and when some of them got loose, we were called in to act as cowboys. There was also a significant Chinese Lutheran congregation in the area, and when a Chinese school was called for, I had to prepare the pine timber which had been salvaged from the old wharf. Despite that fact that most of the nails had been removed, enough had been missed for me to have to learn how to sharpen and re-gullet the saws.

I also remember the time a ship, the *Simbang* brought lumber to rebuild a house at Biliau, a village without a wharf. The ship therefore anchored offshore, and we cast the timber overboard preparatory to floating it to shore. It sank! It was Australian hardwood. We therefore had to buoy it up with pine, and drag it ashore with canoes. This hardwood was a new experience for us Americans. Nails bent when you hammered them in; you had to first drill a hole – and even then, take care that the bit didn't break. It blunted the saws so much, I had to learn a new way of sharpening them.

Another time, a local copra ship went to Karkar Island, near Madang, and ended up on the reef. A group of therefore took our petrol engine and water pump to the ship, and helped pump out enough water to allow the high tide to lift it off.

Ultimately, at the beginning of July, we were able to commence the work that was to occupy us for the rest of our stay: building the Yagaum Hospital. In fact, some of our group stayed on as lay workers to finish the construction about 1951. By then it was the best in the country, under the overall control of Dr Brown, a man who could perform remarkable feats with his hands. Back in Finchhafen, I had watched him set and screw the broken arm of a traffic accident victim, and on another occasion, remove a patient's spleen.

To be situated midway between Madang and Amele, the hospital could be reached only by means of a dirt road and a ford across the brackish Gum River, which even then was accessible only a low tide. The whole convoy of equipment had to be unloaded and walked through the river, and the vehicles driven across, before being washed out with fresh water to prevent rust. (Ultimately, Russell Scherer managed to put a bridge across it, and things got speeded up.) At last we came to a stretch of completely cleared ground completely covered with gluey red mud, immediately calling for the epithet of "Mud Hill". The mud clinging glutinously to our boots, we arrived at a bush hut fifteen feet by twenty. These are your quarters, boys! And you thought the warehouse at Lae was primitive! Here all our bunks were pushed against each other at the back of the hut; we had to climb over our neighbours' to get to our own. The front served as a dining area and kitchen, complete with native cook boy. After a month we moved into four new prefabricated huts intended for medical orderlies.

Also provided was an outdoor shower, created by the simple expedient of filling a 20-gallon drum with hot water, and raising it with a cord. The bottom of the drum was fitted with a shower head, which could be turned on and off. However, the pieces of two-by-fours which covered the floor had to be approached with care, because they were a favourite lurking place for scorpions. This gave one of our crew a bright idea. He got hold of an old magneto, and extended two wires into the showers. One you were inside, he would give it a quick flick, and you would jump from the mild electric shock, and imagine you had been stung by a scorpion.

Yagaum Hospital had been designed by an architect, and each member of the crew was assigned a separate task in its construction. Mine was to prepare the timber in a workshop on the other side of a nearby gully. I had a bench saw powered by a large petrol engine, and a 60 cm sizing machine, along with various electric lights powered by the hospital's own power plant. With the aid of unskilled native staff, I was required to prefabricate doors, studs, and trusses over thirty feet long. To erect the trusses, we made a big A frame, and put them on a jeep. As the jeep lifted them off the ground and raised them on top of the plates, they were bolted and nailed in place. Lots of other challenges would come our way, and whenever they did, they crew would get together to work out a plan of action. These days, everything is mechanised, but seventy years ago it was all hard manual labour.

Madang had its diversions. Because we had little money, we were granted permission to make and sell folding chairs for the local R.S.L. [Returned Servicemen's League] club in our free time. We also did a certain amount of swimming, as well as having the use of a dugout canoe fitted with a sail and an outrigger. A big treat was to go into Madang and watch the movies at the Tropical Theatre, the name applied to a roof and half-walls of corrugated iron, a screen, and benches dug into the ground, surrounded by palm trees. Of course, to get there, we had to negotiate the Gum River. Where it debouched into the sea, the fast-moving mixture of fresh and salt water used to stir up marine phosphorescence, which in turn attracted both sharks and crocodiles. We were warned never to ford the Gum at high tide, at night. But one evening we had no choice, because two friends and I had inadvertently stayed too late in Madang. The first man waded through, and found himself up to his neck. Arriving at the other side, and panning his torch around, he called out that he had seen a crocodile – a small one, admittedly, but a crocodile never the less. Suddenly, before my eyes – for I was number three - the second fellow disappeared under the water. Had a crocodile taken him? No, he had just tripped on a fallen tree. And to add to it all, we had to hike back soaking wet. Needless to say, we took a lot more care of the time and the tides in future, and we were glad when Russell finally built his bridge.

As our stay in New Guinea neared its end, we were granted a excursion into the Highlands as furlough. Harry Vorrath, David Krueger, and Doug Kohn, the one Australian in our crew, were my companions. A mission plane flew us into Raipinka, where we helped butcher a cow for Christmas, and acquired some horses from Rev. Frerichs, and commenced our 200 mile, 20 day walk to Mt Hagen. It really opened our eyes. No road led over the range from Asaroka, only a foot track too steep for horses to be ridden. I remember clinging to the tail of my mount as we went up, and when arrived, we sent the horses back. Down the other side, we beheld the Chimbu River churning down through a high rock wall, a section of which had fallen down to create a natural bridge. From there we passed down to Ega, thence to Omkalai, where we watched people making salt in the Wahgi Valley. By night, we stayed in the houses of the *kiaps*, or patrol officers, or even in the houses of the natives, who always welcomed us. In fact, often the native houses were more rainproof than those of the kiaps.

Salt is such a part of everyday life, that we forget that, to most primitive, inland communities it is as precious as gold. Much of the cleared ground of New Guinea is covered by blady grass known as *kunai* (pronounced "coon–eye"): tall grass with edges made sharp by embedded silica, which cut the hands which grasp it and the legs that pass through. But these people would burn it, then run spring water through the ashes, and boil it dry, till a small residue of salt lay at the bottom. This was repeated, laboriously, time and again, until very large plates of salt six inches thick resulted. It was their trade item – so valuable to the purchasers that it formed part of the bride price.

At this point it might be useful to digress, and explain some basic New Guinean customs, because they will form the background of the rest of this history. "Bride price" is our term, not theirs, and is somewhat of a misnomer. Our own custom of the bride's family paying for the wedding is the last vestige of the dowry system, still extant in traditional parts of Europe, but nobody calls the dowry a bridegroom price. The fact is, in primitive horticultural societies such as those of Africa and Melanesia, which use the hoe, women do a great deal – sometimes the majority – of work in the fields. Daughters are an economic asset, so the bridegroom must compensate her family for her loss. In urban areas, and agricultural societies based on the plough, a daughter is an economic liability, and her father must pay the groom a dowry to take her off his hands.

Marriage is expected to be a family and community affair. Our own custom of wedding gifts and bridal showers is meant to help the newlyweds set up their first home. It is gradually losing its function in the affluent society, as more and more young people can afford to live independently before marriage. If both are living independently, the issue becomes, not acquiring possessions for the joint home, but of getting rid of duplicates. In New Guinea, when a man wants a wife, his family goes out to find one for him. Usually, the couple will know each other, at least by reputation, and the consent of both the couple and both sets of parents is required. The families then negotiate the bride price, in the form of salt, pigs, money, spades, axes, shells, and other such items. As the years have passed, the price has changed, but not the principle. If a divorce occurs, the bride price must be returned – and half of that has already been consumed. The result is a strong pressure from all the relatives, at least on the bride's side, to make the marriage work. Considering the number of broken marriages in our own society, I often feel we ought to develop something similar.

The economic system also permits something less desirable: widespread polygamy. In later years I was to meet a man who, like the well-known man from St Ives, who had seven wives. This sort of thing is possible because the wives can virtually support themselves. Nevertheless, only a minority of marriages are polygamous. The husband, after all, has to provide a bride price for the second wife. It also leaves some other man without a wife – or it would, if warfare didn't remove the surplus males, as used to happen in the olden days.

In an earlier paragraph I mentioned pigs and shells. Not many people realize that the word "fee" comes from an Indo-European word meaning "cattle". Two or three thousand years ago, our own ancestors counted their wealth in cattle, as the Africans still do. In Melanesia it is pigs, and the community leaders in the Highlands, the so-called "big men" are those who have discovered how to manipulate the pig market. A budding entrepreneur will borrow a pig, pay it back with a piglet as interest, raise the other piglets, hire labour with the promise of a piglet, and with other, similar activities, develop a significant herd, while at the same time exchanging various other consumer goods until he is the richest man in the village. There is nothing our Wall St tycoons could teach these Stone Age capitalists when it comes to wheeling and dealing.

However, although livestock have the advantage of breeding faster than compound interest, they are nevertheless cumbersome, and not easily divisible. For that, you need something small and portable, but at the same time precious by virtue of being both rare, and desirable as ornamentation. In Europe, this meant silver and gold. In the highlands of New Guinea, the answer was the *kina* ("kee-na"), the lustrous mother-of-pearl of the gold lip oyster (*Pinctada maxima*), as large as a dinner plate, and imported along the narrow, strife-ridden jungle pathways all the way from the coast. A single kina could buy a piglet; twelve would buy an adult pig. Under the Australian administration, the official exchange rate was one kina to twelve shillings, or about two weeks' wages for a native worker. Such was its importance in the early days, that when Papua New Guinea finally became independent, they called their currency the Kina.

Climate also affects national temperament. Western civilisation, with its work ethic and inventiveness, has been forged by the presence of a hard winter, which both necessitates and enables the storage of food during the productive months. The tale of the grasshopper and the ant is fundamental to European culture. In the tropics, however, nature is bountiful, provided one is prepared to put in the required effort. But food will not keep. The only way to handle a surplus is to consume it in a big, slap-dash party to which everyone is invited – with the understanding that you will also be invited the next time your neighbour has a surplus. Thus, much of the community life of Papua New Guinea revolves around the giving of periodic feasts.

But to continue – at Ega, in Chimbu we were welcomed

by Pastor Wilhelm Bergmann, the first missionary to that area, having arrived in 1929, or three years before the Leahy brothers. (He was also German, but I do not know how he passed the war. Probably he had been interned.) Those early missionaries had a hard time. Here at Chimbu, Pastor Bergmann had made things work, and he produced nearly everything he needed. He grew his own vegetables, raised his own cattle, produced his own milk, made excellent sausages, and even made his own wine. We enjoyed our stay at his centre, and then moved on to Kerowagi Station.

Here we were met with the impressive sight of a grove of magnificent blue gum trees, native to the area. Not only that, they were taboo to the local population; no-one dared lay an axe against them, for they believed they were the abode of the dead. It wasn't the universal belief. In some places, people spoke of the dead going to Oiboku, a high mountain in the Banz region, but at Banz itself, the mission station had been erected on an old burial ground, and we found a grove of oaks sacred to the departed. Superstition, of course, but ask yourself: what do you feel in the presence of huge, majestic trees? Our own ancestors sensed them to be numinous with a power beyond the human. The oracular oaks of Dodona, the sacred groves of the druids, the oak sacred to Thor, which St Boniface felled when he defied the gods of the Hessians – all speak of the awe of the vast primeval forests felt by those forced to eke out their existence on its fringe.

To get to Mt Hagen, we had to cross the Wahgi River on a swaying bridge of vines. Several years later, when I journeyed to the lower Wahgi Valley in the company of Pastor R. Heuter, we had to wait a day while the local people replaced a similar bridge worn out with age, so I may as well describe it here. The lawyer vines grow in the mountains to a great length, and as thick as a man's thumb. Three sets of vines were passed across the river in the shape of a triangle. A cable of three or four, woven together, formed the base. Another cable went across on either side at chest height. Finally, after the three main vine cables had been interconnected by a whole web of shorter vines, it was ready for the stout hearted traveler to cross over, treading on the swaying base, clinging to the rails on either side, and trying not to gaze down at the turbulent water. Repairing an existing bridge is one thing; throwing the initial bridge across must have required real ingenuity. At Banz the river was wide, but further downstream, in the Bomai area, the gorge was very deep and narrow, and the river roared as it dropped hundreds of feet per mile to the coast.

On the trail, the people were friendly, and were quite happy to exchange the goods we carried – shells, salt, matches, and the like – for food. A young pig might cost us a kina shell, and maybe an axe. Whereas the coastal houses were built on posts to allow for cooling, in the mountains they hugged the ground for warmth. And, in case you are wondering, in both areas, a small bamboo shack with a very narrow hole in the ground served as a lavatory. Also, unlike the coast dwellers, with their laplaps, or wrap-around skirts of European cloth, the Highlanders still dressed in their traditional fashion. At Mt Hagen, the women were naked but for grass skirts, while the loins of the men were protected by woven nets in front, and in the rear, by a cluster of tanget grass called *asgras* ("arse grass") in Pidgin. Special occasions, however, called for more elaborate decoration: body paint, mother of pearl, boar's tusks, the bones of bats, and a multicoloured panoply of feathers from the birds of paradise – a magnificent, barbaric splendour which has since become the signature of the Highlands.

In Banz and Mt Hagen we saw men carrying bows and arrows, and spears taller than themselves. Some bore shields of hoop pine wood, as wide as themselves and half as high, and a full inch in thickness. Shield in one hand, and a stone club or axe in the other, they would go into battle with an archer bringing up the rear. White people had little to fear from violence, but the authorities had their hands full controlling inter-tribal fighting. Quarrels over land, or women, or even the belief that one group had used sorcery against the other, would

43

set village against village. Not surprisingly, many of the mission stations had been built on neutral ground between hostile groups. But fighting in the Highlands was not like the American Indian warfare we had been brought up on – no midnight raids, ambushes, or skulking in the forest. It was as ritualised as a football match, only deadlier. The two teams would line up, shouting and posturing, before letting loose with spears and arrows, then clubs and axes, and usually finishing after the first couple of casualties. Amazingly enough, Clarence Wegenast and Russell Boerger, who did the Highlands tour separately from us, actually blundered onto one of these tribal battles, and got a ringside view.

A Gypsy Moth biplane flew us out of Mt Hagen. The pilot had to start it by cranking the propeller, and as we trundled down the runway, we became increasingly concerned as the tree line loomed up ahead of us. As we finally rose into the air, we felt we could almost reach out and touch the treetops. "Well," said the pilot, when we reached home base, "we were a bit overloaded, but it looks like we made it."

Our two and a half years were over, and all of us had been changed. All around us we had witness the desperate physical needs of the church, and the desperate spiritual needs of hundreds of thousands of people who, through no fault of their own, lived in savagery and ignorance, outside of salvation. Of the ten volunteers, six either stayed on in New Guinea, or returned later to the mission field – and I was one of the latter. It was in New Guinea that I finally received my call to the ministry. Once I had looked upon the ministry as a career; now it would be a vocation. I had thought to work for the church in America; instead, I would work for the Lord in New Guinea.

In April 1949, just before Easter, the *Duntroon* sailed out of New Guinea with me as a passenger heading home. My companions were Harry Vorrath and Clarence Wegenast, two of the volunteers, a missionary's daughter, Jenny Maahs, and one of our superiors, Harvey Hildebrand, on a stretcher due to a back injury, and accompanied by his wife. There was still time for one last bit of tomfoolery. As the only volunteer with the foresight to bring along clippers, comb and scissors, I had been the team's barber, but now I sported a beard of my own. But while I lay asleep on board, Harry and Clarence decided a red beard would be just the thing to set off my Atebrin-yellow face, and when I awoke, I found my whiskers had been dyed with Mercurochrome. So, once we were in Sydney, it was off to the hospital for Harvey, off to the People's Palace for the rest of us, and then off to the barber for me.

We now discovered that someone had forgotten to confirm our reservations back to the States, and our bookings had been given to others. We were stuck in Sydney again! That city sure didn't like its visitors getting away! Not only that, but we had nowhere to stay. Easter was coming up, and all the hotels had been pre-booked by country folk arriving for the Easter Show. I can't remember where the womenfolk got accommodation, but it is likely they were put up by Doug Kohn's family, who lived in Sydney. But what about the rest of us? Pastor Stolz was contacted, and his wife told us they had floor space and extra mattresses, if we wanted to stay with them.

Anybody objectively looking back over his or her life will realize that, at crucial points, it turns on small events which the world calls chance or luck, but the wise recognize as being scripted by a Higher Power. When I left New Guinea, I had my life all mapped out in my head. As far as I could see, this was just one small glitch on that road.

Then I met the pastor's 18 year old daughter.

Chapter 3
The Pastor's Daughter
Theophila's Story

South Australia's Eyre Peninsula must be as far removed from the American world view as Nebraska is from Australians' - and mostly off the horizon of other Australians, in any case. Separated from the state capital by two deep gulfs, with an annual rainfall of only 14 inches [35 cm], it is officially semi-desert. These days, the shoreline is dotted with the holiday units of Adelaide-ites, but on 17 July 1930, when I was born to Regina Stolz née Wallent and Pastor Christoph Wilhelm Stolz, it was pretty much the back of beyond, and the little inland town of Cleve was even further "beyond".

I wasn't actually born in Cleve. Mother objected to the local doctor and hospital, and ensured that I came into the world in the Tumby Bay Hospital. My sister, Christobelle arrived two years later, and Rosalind three years after her. Nobody could label our family background as run-of-the-mill. My father's four brothers were all pastors, one even reaching the rank of President, the Lutheran equivalent of bishop, and three of his four sisters married pastors. Their own father was the General President in charge of the whole United Evangelical Lutheran Church of Australia – and he was not the only pastor in his generation. As for Dad, his parish spread over most of the Eyre Peninsula, from Kimba in the north, south to Port Lincoln, and west to Ceduna, on the Nullarbor. It was not a calling a man would take for love of money. When I grew up, my first pay was greater than his! Often, his stipend was supplemented with produce donated by the parishioners.

Let us be clear about one thing: despite our German surname and our use of German in the home, we were not German. My sisters and I were the fourth generation born in Australia, and King George and his Empire had no more loyal supporters than the Stolz family.

Life in the old parsonage was primitive even by the standards of the time. Lamps and candles took the place of electric lighting. Water came from an underground tank, a manual pump being used to transfer it to a smaller tank near the kitchen. A wood stove served for cooking, and on washing day another wood fire was built under a copper vat known, appropriately, as the "copper". Once the water was hot enough, you just added clothes and soap, and stirred with a big wooden pole, after which the clothes would be fed through a hand-operated wringer and squeezed dry. But water was always scarce. At bath time a portable round tub was brought out, and we three children took turns in the same water each evening. We cleaned our teeth with a cup of water – no more. Finally, the water would be poured down a drain, next to which Mother grew excellent rhubarb.

Refrigeration – forget it! Perishables received short term storage in what we called the "pantry", but which was actually a cellar approached down three steps, with water-soaked cloths lining the concrete floor. It might be added, however, that towards the end of our stay in Cleve, refrigeration did arrive, but it was far too expensive for the likes of us. It was not till the end of the war, when we moved to Sydney, that we were introduced to the luxury of an ice box.

Of course, it goes without saying that indoor sewage was something only the silvertails at the big end of the big city could expect. A small shack in the backyard had to do for the rest of the population. In the cities, the pan would be collected every week by an honest workman considered socially inferior to the garbage collector. Out in the country, the shack was mounted over a deep hole in the ground, while newspapers or magazines served the function of the soft roll now familiar to the modern generation.

Virtually every summer the harsh, semi-desert sky was blackened with the smoke of bush fires, up to seven burning at once. And every year, the same sky was darkened by grasshopper plagues, and by the fires, made of bran and some other ingredient, lit by the farmers to drive them away. Nevertheless, the dry, semi-desert air, and the absence of city-light glare left the night sky clear and bright. During the 1930s we must also have passed through a special sunspot phase because, just as Leon experienced in the Northern Hemisphere, our night time rambles were frequently made glorious by the play of the aurora.

At age five, I was commenced at the two-room Cleve Primary School. One room housed classes four to eight, while Miss Ilene Elson took the lower grades. A male teacher took the upper grades: Frederick Bell being the one I remember most, but also the great, fat headmaster, Mr Clark. Spelling and multiplication were learned by rote repetition, and when the boys were learning woodwork, Miss Elson was teaching the older girls the domestic arts of cooking, laundry, sewing, and darning. (Darning is the lost art of repairing holes in socks. I doubt if any member of the younger generation learns it these days.) We even had cast iron "Mrs Potts" irons, which had to be heated on a wood stove before they could be put to use on the clothes. We also had singing and music, and at one point I was the sergeant major of the fife band, but I hardly ever joined in the country dancing lessons. Like Leon's parents, mine regarded dancing as some sort of sin.

For discipline, Mr Clark would call the culprits to the front of the class, and make them touch their toes, before he applied the cane to the seat of their pants. But I don't remember girls ever getting the cane. What I do remember was staying in after school, to be presented by Mr Ball with mathematical problems of division and/or multiplication with numbers long enough to make our hearts quake. But at least we learned something.

Because German was our home language, Mother was determined that we be proficient in English. After church on Sunday she used to give us a spelling bee of twenty words, and if our performance were adequate, she would take us on an outing up the dry creek bed or up the hill, where she was expert in finding scorpions and centipedes. Yes, we were familiar with centipedes – Cleve had really big ones, which used to crawl into the parsonage and give us a scare – but on the hills, among the rocks, Mother liked to turn over stones to see what was underneath. We were also permitted to explore the bush by ourselves, looking for beautiful things, such as the orchids encountered here and there. I remember the sighing of the winds through the she-oaks, and the feel of the fallen needles under our shoes, as we slid on them. In season, we were also allowed to wander the Rifle Range, whence the sheep had been removed, and gather mushrooms. We also, believe it or not, had three pet emus while at the old parsonage, and a pet galah which could say my name. (In those days, there were very few restrictions on keeping native animals.) At Christmas time friends sometimes allowed us the use of an iron shack next to the beach at Arno Bay, the port for the district's wheat and wool, and we could pretend we were holidaying at a seaside resort.

Santa Claus never visited our house, any more than he did Leon's. However, a tree would be erected by our parents, but we were not allowed to see it until it was decorated, and we were lead to believe that the *Christkind*, or Christ Child would arrive at Christmas, and would expect us to have been good. Apparently, He takes the place of St Nicholas in many parts of Germany and Austria. But it was at Easter that things got really interesting, for then the *Osterhase*, or Easter Bunny came visiting. At various times in the lead-up to Easter, we would find bunny tracks on the gravel pathway beside our verandah, leading to the back of the house, where he (? she) would leave an egg in the nest we had make for him, and perhaps eat the carrot we had provided. On Easter Day itself, there would be more tracks, and a whole collection of eggs, both traditionally boiled and dyed ones, and the new chocolate variety. Of course, it was Dad who made the rabbit tracks, but he had us completely fooled. Once, he was called outside to talk to someone, and on his return, told us it was the Easter Bunny. Incredibly enough, I believed this tradition right up to the time I went to college.

Sunday school was not considered necessary for the pastor's children, for our parents were able to teach us at home, following the little text cards printed for children, and memorising Luther's Small Catechism. When Dad was visiting the distant congregations of his parish, we stayed home with Mother, who read out the liturgy, and one of Luther's extra long sermons. As we grew older, we were able to read the lessons and sing the hymns – all the time seated on the horrible scratchy sofa Mother's parents had given her.

However, when services were to be held at Crossville, Yadnarie, and Cowel, we could go along. Crossville was a real trial. Because of the distance, the service was invariably held in the afternoon, when the summer sun and flies were particularly bad, two girls in the front pews used to turn around and gawk at us, and Mother was always ready with a pinch on the knee if we failed to sit still on the hard, uncomfortable seats. On the other hand, I loved going to the church on the hill at Yadnarie. While members of the congregation stopped to discuss matters with Dad after the service, we could gaze out for miles over the farmlands, as far as Mt Pristiller. When the land was fallow, the air would shimmer with the heat, and swirl into short-lived "dust devils" or "willy willies". At Cowel lived a special friend, the young organist, Delores Zanker, with her long, curling locks. She worked at the telephone exchange at Cowel, and quickly let us know about an attempt to burn down our church during the Second World War. We still exchange cards at Christmas.

Even so, when I was still quite young – probably still in the lower grades – I was often left to tend to my younger sisters after school. Mother used to feel for all the lonely women on the distant properties, and so would accompany Dad on his circuits. At those times, we would often surprise her by cleaning the kitchen from canisters to floor, using the skills taught at school. If their stay extended into the night, I would often spend the whole time deep in a book. But one time they failed to show up after a funeral at Lock, and I became desperate. They should have been back hours before, and the only explanation I could latch onto was some terrible accident. As it turned out, I was half right. When they finally staggered home in the wee hours of the morning, they explained that the car had become hopelessly mired in mud many miles from home, and every attempt at digging it out only made the matter worse, until they were left with no recourse but to trudge back on foot.

People of today cannot imagine what the roads were like on the Eyre Peninsula, particularly those between Lock, Cummins, and Cleve. When I was still very young, and Christobelle still a babe in arms, we were required to do a night drive. For some reason, I wanted to sit in the back seat, but my parents were adamant that I sit between them in the front, where it was warmer. (Those were the days before seat belts were invented.) The moon was full as we opened the dog gate and passed through the dingo fence, and down into a hollow. Suddenly, a dazzled kangaroo appeared in the headlights, and the next moment, it made a wild attempt to bound over, or past the car. It landed right in my mother's lap, which was also occupied by baby Christobelle, and then jumped into the back seat. Everything happened at once. Dad stopped the car, opened the door, and the 'roo hopped out. The baby was crying, and the moonlight told us she was bleeding profusely. Either the kangaroo's claws, or a shard of glass had slashed her left cheek and her neck, leaving her jugular vein visible. The only more or less sterile dressings which could be found at short notice were some freshly ironed handkerchiefs. To compound the emergency, after a slow, cold return journey, we found that the doctor's hands were shaking so much, that he had to wait until morning to stitch the wounds. But Chrissy survived, though she has borne the scars most of her life.

Another time, Dad drove to Lock in an Oakland car, and

returned home quite literally on the spokes of the wheel. There were simply no more tyres left, and the marks of the spokes could be followed back along the rain-drenched road.

Years later, after we had moved into the new parsonage on Hospital Hill, and had exchanged the Oakland for a Chevrolet, we were traveling to Cummins along an all weather road. This made a great change from some of the terrible thoroughfares we normally had to put up with, but it was certainly not bitumenised. We three girls were in the back. Mother wanted to open the window, and grabbed the wrong handle. The Chevrolet's doors opened forward rather then back. The next instance, Rosalind screamed as we saw her fall out of the door, and being dragged along the road. Ultimately, she was admitted to Tumby Bay Hospital with bruising and severe gravel rash. However – and this might surprise the younger generation – in those days, despite the heat and the discomfort, women wore corsets, and on this occasion it saved her from an even worse battering.

On one occasion at school, some VIP – probably an inspector – arrived, and I was asked to stand up and speak German for him. It was considered a novelty at the time, but after the war broke out when I was nine years old, it became a mark of suspicion. Even so, we never expected the crises which swept through the family in 1940. In June Dad was sent to Sydney on various projects, but primarily to assist another pastor. Mother was still all on her own when, in late August or early September I came down with a streptococcal throat infection. This was no minor childhood illness. I was desperately sick. Our home was placed under quarantine – although Mr Ball, the teacher did not hesitate to visit, and the doctor came every day. Death hovered constantly at my bedside, and for one dreadful night it appeared he would claim me, but by virtue of the prayers of my family, and the new sulphanilamide drugs, I survived.

Even when the crisis was over, and it was decided I

needed a tonsillectomy at Adelaide's Calvary Hospital, I was so sick that, to this day, I cannot remember how I got there. No doubt I flew on Guinea Airways, which used to service the Eyre Peninsula. What I do remember was being placed in the same room as my father's aunt, Mrs Reidel. By this time, Dad had returned from Sydney, and he took me home. This time, we caught the S.S. *Minippa* from Port Adelaide to Port Lincoln, where we switched to his car for the drive north to Cleve. Suddenly, out of the north came a terrible dust storm – nothing unusual in those parts. Visibility was almost zero, but we pressed on. Finally, when the sky was clear, we stepped out to view the results, we found the windscreen and the whole of the front had been effectively sand-blasted by the gravel swept up from the road, and the paint had been completely removed from the mudguards.

It was during this trip that Dad complained of the feeling of gravel in his eyes. That was in September. On 9 October he left for Adelaide again to consult an eye specialist. Glaucoma was floated as a possible diagnosis though, at this date, I suspect that, had it been present, it would have been secondary to some other eye disease. In any case, he was ordered to return home and rest his eyes.

On 17 October he was sitting in the Guinea Airways office, intending to book a flight home, when a police officer called him out, and announced, "I have in my possession a Warrant for your detention; it is called a Detention Order."

"How unique!" he replied, and began to laugh. Because of various events back home, he was not surprised. The Detention Order had been made out on 2nd October; they had taken that long to find him. The military officials drove him to his father's home, where he was able to collect his belongings.

"Can you give me any reason for you being interned?" the policeman finally asked.

"Yes," he responded, "two men have got me set and I know that they have said all sorts of things about me, things that are not true. All of the Returned Soldiers at Cleve are with me with the exception of two, one of which is named Pratt and I know that he has done everything to harm me."

"Can you prove all you say?"

"Yes, I think I can." He then added: "I have also heard that some of them have even made bets that I would be interned."[3]

The first thing we knew about it was a rat-a-tat on the front door early one morning. A policeman and, I think, a representative of the R.S.L., had come to search the house. My poor mother was frantic, and in tears, as they went through the house from top to bottom, even tearing up the floorboards in a futile search for contraband or a transmitter. Tante Anna, Mother's aunt, was with us at the time, and she became a tower of strength. As this was the only time she ever visited, I am sure God had sent her to her for just this purpose.

Perhaps the bureaucracy was not deliberately malicious, just callous. No-one worried about the fate of an internee's family; we could all have starved, for all they cared. Not only was there no money coming in, but our bank account was frozen, and we were forced to live from hand to mouth. The image of boiled cucumbers is firmly implanted in my memory of that time.

Not only that, but we quickly became social lepers. The community naturally assumed that there must have been some good reason for the internment and, in any case, anyone who associated with us would also be tainted with suspicion. The church fathers did little to assist us, and we children were alone at school. Bit by bit, however, our true friends gathered round, though they had to be careful about it. We will always bless Fred and Sylvia Ball, the headmaster and his wife, for their unfailing kindness, and also Miss Elson, the teacher of the lower grades. Then, one day, one of the local grocers came

[3] Report by police officer S. G. McKay 17.10.40, included as an appendix to a B Th research paper by Tim Jarick (1997) entitled, *Was the Internment of Lutheran Pastors During the Second World War Due to an Active Policy of "Deutschtum" Within the Church?"*, Luther Seminary, North Adelaide, S.A.

around and asked Mother how she was managing for food. She had to tell him that we were in dire straits. In that case, he suggested she make a list of everything we needed, and she could settle accounts at a later date.

Meanwhile, Dad was held in solitary confinement at Keswick Military Barracks, without any reading material at all, not even his Bible. He was effectively left to stare into space for two months. Apart from discussions with his legal counsel, the only respite was during the daily exercise period, during which he took the opportunity to share the gospel with one of the other internees, and bring him to Christ.

But, even in wartime, a citizen cannot be imprisoned without appeal to *habeas corpus*. On 3rd December, he was brought before the National Security Advisory Committee for the hearing of his objection to the order of detention. At one point, when a piece of paper fell down from the magistrate's desk, he picked it up and discovered he could read it. The enforced rest given to his eyes in prison had cured them! As the hearing proceeded, a petition for his release was produced, submitted by a Methodist minister, the Rev. W.F. Clarke and containing 290 signatures from people of every denomination and ethnic origin. Several witnesses who had known him for 13 to 15 years, mostly Anglo-Saxon non-Lutherans, came forth to testify to his loyalty to King and Empire. It was told how he took part in the local Progress Association, the Institute, Civil Defense League, and Hospital Board, but that his organization of the local Red Cross Branch had met fierce hostility from a rival group headed by a Mr P. J. Sampson.

The Committee also received a denunciation prepared by the same P. J. Sampson, with six other signatures by people who did not know Dad personally. A constable had also made "discrete enquiries", and came up with a number of anonymous denunciations in quite general terms. They were not impressed. To quote the official report:[4]

---

[4] Report of the The National Security Advisory Committee, 12.12.40 *in*

The Committee in the present case is again faced with the difficulty of deciding between anonymous Reports containing few or no concrete facts on the one hand and the evidence upon oath of obviously honest witnesses subjected to cross-examination on the other hand.

They were also completely unimpressed with one piece of evidence tendered by the prosecution. Dad had written a letter to a soldier, in which he said, "As we serve 'our King and Empire' so let us not forget to serve the King of Kings and Lord of Lords," and which he ended with the salutation: "Yours in the Master's service."

The Committee [the report stated] sees no justification for attributing to the words "Master". "King of Kings" or "Lord of Lords" veiled references to Hitler.

Great rejoicing reigned in our household when we heard that Dad was coming home. He arrived back on Christmas Eve, bringing a special present for us girls: a toy car we could drive around the spare block in make-believe adventures.

Nevertheless, he was required to report to the police once a week, and give a week's notice to police if he intended to leave the area, and this cross was not lifted from his shoulders until 1942. Even so, the most wonderful thing about the whole ordeal was that his eyes had been cured, and God had used him to bring another victim to salvation – and what brief suffering can count against that?

Of the seven men who denounced him, one died shortly afterwards, and the the others came in, bit by bit, to apologize. The last one went to Sydney specifically to apologize, but having no actual knowledge as to Dad's location. As it turned out, they happened to meet on a public street , and he knelt down then and there to ask his forgiveness.

With life back to normal, I repeated grade seven in 1942,

Jarick, *op.cit.*

and at the end of the following year, won a scholarship to continue my education. In those days, you must understand, high school was neither compulsory nor normal. Most people left school for work at age thirteen or fourteen. And it went without saying that no high school existed in the whole of Eyre Peninsula, so it was off to the "mainland" and Adelaide for me. Immanuel College, the church school was the obvious choice. However, the college had been commandeered by the Air Force, so where was the education of the students to take place? A beautiful home with fine gardens and spacious grounds had been purchased in North Walkerville, with a ballroom which could be used as an assembly point, and enough space for classrooms, meals, sports grounds, and male student quarters. The girls were accommodated in two other lovely early homes in the same suburb, and in our first year the church added a sleep-out for an extra 26 girls, including me. But we had a lot of walking to do.

The lower half of the outer walls of this sleep-out were of fibro (ie impregnated with asbestos), while the top half was of shuttered screens, so there was not much separating us from the weather. The shutters would be left open during the stifling hot summer months, and when a storm came up during the night, the prefects would have to get up and close them all. Early one morning, after a night of heavy storms, with hail, we were in the main college building when it was struck by lightning – a frightening experience one never forgets.

On the other hand, the larger hostel had well-planned gardens and lawns, an attractive tennis court, and many out buildings which could be used for various purposes, such as a music room. The verandas were all enclosed with canvas, which could be rolled down for privacy and protection from the weather. Sleeping there was not too bad. But in 1945, when I was staying in those quarters, there was an outbreak of scarlet fever, and some sections went into quarantine. Initially, I thought I had escaped, but when I returned home, the fever struck as a macabre Christmas present. My hair fell out and my skin peeled. On Christmas Eve we sisters were at home while our parents attended a service at Cowell, when we were suddenly hit by a ferocious dust storm, full of thunder and lightning, but without rain, and that was one time I distinctly remember being   scared.

In 1946, orders came to transfer to Sydney, to "put the Lutheran church on the map". I can't remember much of the trip, except that it was undertaken in the family Chevrolet, with the three girls in the back, and the space between Mother and Dad in the front being occupied by Pinnippy, our beautiful Major Mitchell cockatoo. Under normal circumstances, she had a stand to perch on, and a chain around her leg, and her main hobby was gnawing on anything her stout little beak could latch onto.

I shall never forget our first morning in Sydney, in the new parsonage. Not only was the heat and humidity oppressive, but I was a country girl, and waking up to the roar of the electric trains and the traffic was something which is etched in my memory.

Throughout my life, I have been constantly amazed at the sort of accommodation parishes consider suitable for a pastor's family. The bathroom-cum-laundry was essentially a single room with the kitchen. Only a plywood partition separated the two, stretching a little more than body-height from the floor; it was possible to hand objects over the top from one room to the other without using the door. Not only that, it was on the main household thoroughfare; one door led in from the dining room, another connected to the bathroom, and another led out to the back, and to a landing leading to our bedroom. Just imagine, washing clothes, cooking, and washing dishes all in that confined space, with people coming an going! On washdays Mother used to be beside herself. In addition, the house came with the following:

- a living room where the coke heater could not be used because it belched smoke;
- a master bedroom exposed to all the traffic noise, and

smelling musty from the moisture;

- a bedroom-cum-study for the three teenage daughters, complete with three narrow beds, wardroom, sewing machine, dressing table, and considerably less room than was necessary to swing a cat;
- a small "confinement room" with bookshelves, two wardrobes, and a bunk bed for particularly trustworthy friends; plus
- Dad's study and interview room, constructed by closing in the small front porch, and which had to be approached by two separate doors. Weatherproof it was not; when the southerlies came, the wind howled through the louvres, and when it rained, water poured in under the floor, and dripped down from the ceiling ruining many of his best books. (Our own bedroom also required an open umbrella on occasions.)

But at least we were now introduced to the luxury of an ice box. A man used to come around regularly to deliver the ice, and Mother organized a roster for us girls to empty the melt water container under the box. If any of us forgot, there was a mess to clean up. Also, we now had an honest-to-goodness flush toilet, albeit in the back yard. Back in Cleve, after my bout with streptococcal throat in 1940, we had been advised to give up the hole in the ground. Instead, we used a simple bucket latrine, and buried the contents in the ground.

Although the parsonage was in Earlwood, Trinity Church was, in fact, situated in George Street, right downtown, not far from Central Station, and the congregation was composed of Estonians, Germans, Latvians, and Finns, as well as Anglo-Saxon Australians. Most Saturday nights the Estonians held some function or other, often leaving a big cleanup to be performed before the Sunday service. As the church hall was on the second floor, to enter meant climbing a long flight of narrow stairs, while facing the smell of garbage from the   fish shop immediately underneath. So dreary was the place, that Mother sought to improve the atmosphere with flowers. Often on Saturdays, therefore, or early Sunday mornings, we would be sent into the bush to obtain greenery to add to the flower arrangements. Visitors often commented on how cheerful the flowers made it.

But I am getting ahead of myself. The first issue was to arrange for our education. Christobelle and Rosalind attended local schools, but I was sent back to Immanuel in Adelaide. Thus, I missed Leon's visit the first time he was stranded in Sydney.

After returning from Adelaide, I went to the Bedford Business College in Sydney, where I studied Pittman shorthand and typing. For those of my readers less than a quarter of a century old, I should explain that, before computers took over the world, typing was performed on bulky, cumbersome devices known as typewriters, for which the nimble fingers of women were considered the most appropriate. If the same letter had to be sent to fifty customers, it had to be typed fifty times, and if a single character were mistyped, the entire page had to be retyped. As you can well imagine, speed and accuracy were considered the mark of a good typist. By the time I left Bedford, I could take shorthand at 120 words a minute, then type it up at 60 words a minute, a skill I had learned to the tune of the "Colonel Bogey March". Even today, I cannot hear that piece of music without thinking: "A.s -D.F.L- K.J.H," but it got me a position as secretary to the Rev. Archie Stuart, secretary for the N.S.W. Branch of the British and Foreign Bible Society.

Meanwhile, almost from his arrival in Sydney, Dad ended up being co-ordinator for missionaries passing to and from New Guinea. So when three lost boys from the mission field turned up on our doorstep that April, it was nothing really out of the ordinary.

"More of the same," I thought.

The Stolz family
Rear: Theophilia (left) and Christobelle
Front: Rosalind between parents, Regina and Christoph

Chapter 4
Love at 9,000 Miles

As mentioned before, the lives of mortals, as often as not, turn on events which fools call chance or luck, and even bigger fools label fate or destiny. Thus, it was by no human planning that several young Americans found themselves stranded in Sydney at the one time no paid accommodation was available. Likewise, although the powers that be made every endeavour to ensure that they were individually able to leave as early as possible, no-one intended that Leon Philippi would end up stranded at the pastor's residence for not quite six weeks. And certainly nobody could have predicted the outcome, least of all the two people involved. Because, between the pastor's daughter in Australia and the farmer's son from Nebraska, there was an almost instant *rapport*.

Make hay while the sun shines, so the proverb goes. Even in 1949, Sydney was a big and exotic city to a boy from the prairies, and here was a teenage girl only too eager to show it to him. We were swept up into the bustle and fanfare of the Royal Easter Show and, of course, there was the standard Harbour cruise, the museum, the art gallery, and so forth. Then there were the migrant camps. Theophila's parents were heavily involved with the Good Neighbour Council, greeting and befriending the new arrivals and assisting them in settling and assimilating – for which her father was later awarded an MBE (Member of the Order of the British Empire). The evenings would often find them driving to nearby camps such as Villawood, and as often as not the back seat would be occupied by the dark-haired daughter of the bush and the sandy-haired son of the plains, holding hands.

Seventy years after the events, do you want to know the full story: the endearments whispered between us, the first kiss, the moonlit strolls down the avenue? The ways of a man with a maid, so the scriptures say, are beyond the understanding of the wisest. Nevertheless, they are the same the world over, and the result is predictable: the average love affair is overwhelmingly exciting to the two people involved, and quite uninteresting to anybody else. If you doubt it, look back at your own courtship. It quickens your blood, no doubt, to think about it, but would anybody else pay to read about it? A natural corollary is that the writers of trashy love stories require a specific plot artifice: to keep the interest of their readers, between the first couple's meeting and the consummation of their romance, they must erect some sort of barrier.

For us, the barrier was obvious and immediate: the Pacific Ocean. More than 9,000 miles separated our respective home towns, and time was running out. No matter how slowly the wheels of bureaucracy turned, they were racing precipitously to the date of Leon's departure. Every embrace was precious. In less than a month and a half, his plane stood waiting. There was a tearful farewell at the airport, and the grim thought that it might really be good-bye, and that we might never see each other again.

Next stop: Fiji, aboard a Lockheed Constellation: triple tail-finned, four-engine propeller driven, little more than half the speed of today's jets, but offering a lot faster return home than the shipbound outward journey, and the latest of elegant design and comfort. The first of the pressurised aircraft, it came complete with bunks for the long trans-oceanic flights. You'd have to be rich to afford that on a jetliner today. There was Leon, pining over the girl he had left behind, but happy that he was at last going home in such comfortable surrounding, when he looked out at the wing. Suddenly, he was aware of smoke and flames issuing from one of the engines. All at once, air travel did not seem such an improvement on sea transport after all. So when they finally landed at the Fijian capital, which is spelled Nadi, but pronounced Nandi, it was announced that they would have to wait while a replacement airliner was brought up from Australia. He was stranded again! This was becoming too much of a routine. At least he had a day's opportunity to see the town, the next plane did take them safely to Hawaii. But only an hour or so out of Honolulu, another engine packed it in. This was definitely not looking good, and it was a very relieved set of passengers who finally deplaned at San Francisco. It was also a very stunned set of parents who met Leon at the station, for they had never set eyes on an Atebrine yellow face before. It took several months before it was back to its natural colour again.

Later, the homecoming crew members were invited to be special guests at a big Luther League youth convention in Pullman, Washington. Clarence Wegenast marched in the parade as a missionary, complete with the sort of pith helmet the team had practically never worn. The rest of the team brought up the van, dressed up as New Guinea natives, beating their *kundus*, or tom-toms, and complete with laplaps and *singsing* regalia. At the following service, each was then presented with a gold-engraved badge.

Now Leon prepared to become an ordained missionary, and the first item on the agenda was to obtain money for a university education. Fortunately, the old high school at Bruning had to be demolished, and high wages were being offered to anyone with experience in the dangerous work of tearing down buildings. Then he worked on the farm, and his father gave him a field of grain for his own use and profit. From there, it was off to Wartburg College in Waverley, Iowa for a Bachelor of Arts degree. It was no pushover. He had to do English three times before he got it right, and Greek was a nightmare.

Here, one might make an aside. Greek, with its complex grammar and its completely foreign alphabet, is the language of the New Testament, and familiarity with it opens a window into the thought patterns of the time. It is essential to anyone who wants to become a theologian. Nevertheless, the fact remains, you can preach the gospel the whole of your life, ministering to the searchers and the soul-sick, without ever having to use a sentence of it. The word of God is not so easily restrained.

Meanwhile, we had started exchanging correspondence. Leon wrote about his difficulties with Greek, and Theophila announced how she was fulling her girlhood ambition to be a nurse, commencing training at the Rachel Forster Hospital in Redfern on 25 May 1949. Particularly popular with her was the children's ward: a cheery place with murals of stories by Pixie O'Hara, and a closed-in place with glass that allowed the outside to be brought inside.

It is while she was there that an incident occurred which has no real bearing on this story, but which nevertheless deserves a mention. Her father has left the utensils for Holy Communion, still in their lined wooden case, in the back seat of his Chevrolet while he was busy in the church. You shouldn't do that in Sydney, even then. When he returned, they were gone, so he immediately walked to the nearby police station to report the theft. But before the police could commence their investigations, the items just as mysteriously reappeared, along with a note from the thief: "Please pray for me." (Which, of course, he did.) Next thing, Theophila was busy in the children's ward, when the battleaxe in charge of the ward came to her with a copy of the *Sydney Morning Herald*. Showing her the report, she asked, she asked if the man in the photo was her dad.

"Well, yes," said Theophila.

"Isn't he a handsome cove?" she replied.

Every so often, at irregular intervals, a messenger would come hurrying up to say that there was an urgent telephone call for Sister Stolz. It would be Leon, calling all the way from America – in the days when STD was a meaningless combination of letters, and communication was by operator-assisted radiophone, with indifferent reception.

"You'll have to talk louder," she'd often cry.

"Are you getting through?" the operator would ask. If we

weren't, the call would be extended gratis until we could. Also, by some fluke or other, Theophila would always be free – taking morning or afternoon tea, or in between handling patients – when the call came, and it always ended with her feeling she was walking on a cloud.

At that time, it should be noted, no-one by Leon had any idea what these long distance telephone calls were costing him. But then, he wasn't buying flowers, or restaurant meals, or facing any of the other expenses courting swains find indispensable.

Absence is to love what wind is to fire: it extinguishes the weak but fans the strong. After two years passed,   Leon made the proposal: would she be his wife, and come with him to New Guinea as a missionary? Of course! But first she consulted her father and mother and, after some prayer and consideration, both parents consented. New Guinea, after all, loomed closer to the Australian horizon than in America. Besides, why shouldn't their daughter head off to some primitive colonial outpost with some foreigner she'd known for just six weeks two years before? It wasn't as if there was anything unreasonable about it!

We became officially engaged on Theophila's 21st birthday, and she set out with her parents to buy an engagement ring with the money Leon had forwarded. As an engagement present, he also sent her a pressure cooker – the first one she'd ever known. Not very romantic, admittedly, but it proved highly useful when dealing with the tough meat of New Guinea. And, you might be interested to know, it is still doing its job. For a while it was non-functional, but when Lois paid a visit in 2008, she brought along some spare parts she'd dug up in Chicago that very year.

That same year, Greek or no Greek, Leon got his B.A. degree. It was time to move on to a Bachelor of Theology course at Wartburg Seminary, Dubuque (not to be confused with Wartburg College, Waverley), but because he had theological differences with one of the   professors, he insisted on transferring to Trinity Seminary in Columbus, Ohio. Another year passed slowly, and a fourth. In 1953 Theophila completed her general nursing, and continued with midwifery at the Royal Women's Hospital in Paddington. Leon was still at Columbus. And yet a fifth year passed.

But all long journeys come to an end. In May 1954, Leon completed his studies. To say he had graduated would be slightly inaccurate. His B.Th. took a while to process – in fact, he was already in New Guinea by the time it caught up with him – but no one doubted that it would come. On 20 June relatives and friends from all over the country flocked to his home town of Bruning for his ordination.

That very morning, before the service began, another ritual took place. Anybody who stays   in New Guinea soon discovers that buses are rare, and railways non-existent, leaving air transport as the predominant, if somewhat hair-raising, method of negotiating the mountains and rivers. For some time, unbeknownst to his family, he had been taking flying lessons. It therefore came as something of a shock to them to learn that he had chosen the day of his ordination for his final practical test. So, for a couple of nail-biting hours, they were left at home while their son and brother soloed in a Super Cub at the Hawks Flying Field, taking off and landing three times by himself. He now had his flying license. It would be an anticlimax, but nevertheless true, to state that that was also the last time he got behind a joystick. Flying turned out to be no more a necessity for his future career than Greek.

After that, things started to move rather rapidly. He was now a Bachelor of Arts, and was soon to be a Bachelor of Theology. It was time to end his bachelor days. Following a wait of another three weeks, his Australian visa came through. After that, with the plaintive strains of "God Be With You Till We Meet Again" in his ears, he took leave of his family, and set was off by land for New Orleans, there to catch a freighter, the *Pioneer Isle* to Australia. No more of those unreliable planes with their combustible engines! How'd you be? A couple of days past the Panama Canal, the steam condenser broke down, adding days to the voyage while they made a new one.

But freighter transport has its advantages. In these days of floating cities disguised as cruise ships, it is the best kept secret of the tourist industry that freighters still offer comfortable and personal passenger service – even for holiday makers. In this case, there were only seven passengers, including a clergyman and his bride on their honeymoon, and a man who had missed his ship – and all his possessions – in Trinidad, and with whom Leon ended up sharing a cabin, and even his shaving gear. But while the condenser was being replaced, the crew strung netting around the deck railing, and converted the deck into a baseball field. The passengers were allowed the run of the ship, and the captain even demonstrated the use of the sextant to Leon. You wouldn't get that sort of service on an ocean liner.

After thirty-nine days at sea, by which time all the fresh food had been exhausted, Leon alighted in Brisbane. It was now 1st September, and only 600 miles and a single day separated us. On the express train to Sydney he was unable to secure a bunk, and was forced to sleep – or at least, attempt to sleep – sitting up. But the railway was solicitous of their passengers' comfort. They halted at intervals for the passengers to use the station cafés (there was no dining car), and to ease the chill of the journey, long metal cylinders filled with hot water were introduced to the cabins. Nevertheless, it was a rather tired and travel-worn American who fell into his fiancée's arms the following day. We had been apart for five years and three and a half months.

Both our families had been supportive, but equally they voiced their concerns. Don't rush into things, they urged us. Take it easy. Get to know each other again before you get married. Good advice, and taken to heart. The wedding wasn't set for another three weeks and two days. Nobody could call that hasty! Theophila's father would officiate, but the Lutheran church above the fish shop was not completely suited for the venue so, in a spirit of inter-denominational good will, the Church of England granted us the use of the 109-year-old Christ Church St Laurence just down the road.

Of course, the wedding would be unusual in that only the bride's side of the family would be represented, but Leon's brother and sisters were determined to send their wishes and blessing just before the big day. It was only then that their father discovered the financial sacrifice his son had been making with all those international telephone calls. The charge was four dollars a minute! You wouldn't pay that much now, and in 1954 money was really worth something. Ernest, Elda, and Lois were required to place four dollars down, cash on the nail, before they lifted the receiver, after which their father stood guard with his eye on the sweep second hand of his watch.

At two p.m. on 25 September, the ten bells of the great sandstone church rang out. There stood the groom, like Moses, a "stranger in a strange land", and wearing a clerical collar for the first time in his life. By his side, as groomsmen, stood his bride's first cousin and his soon-to-be sister-in-law's soon-to-be fiancé, both holding only one white glove and trying to hide the fact that they were one pair short. Down the aisle walked his bride, accompanied in pink by her younger sisters as bridesmaids, and still younger godchild as flower girl. Our hearts were overflowing.

Need we say more? Our honeymoon was in the Blue Mountains, the famed "playground of Sydney", where both of our daughters were later to honeymoon. On our return, our time was taken up preparing for the trip to New Guinea. The mission wanted us there as early as possible, but were told that we needed time to ourselves. On the evening of 2 November, we flew out.

Thus, just sixty days after being reunited, we were

husband and wife, and setting off for a wild new country, without any plans to return. You have to be young and in love!

Chapter 5
Off the Deep End in New Guinea
Theophila's Story

Of course, one shouldn't be over-concerned with earthly glory. Just the same, let me record the opinion that whatever earthly glories accrues to the mission field tends to be concentrated on the male missionary, to the neglect of his wife, who not only provides back-up support, but also plays an active role in mission activities themselves. When we boarded the plane that evening in November, I realised that, as a bride of just five weeks, I was about to be thrown off the deep end into a strange new world. The following day – for aircraft were slower then – saw us in Lae: hot,   humid, and oppressive, full of unaccustomed sights and smells, riotous with the most gorgeous flowers I had ever seen – at the same time, uncomfortable, intimidating, and exhilarating.

Representatives of the mission met us at the airport, and transported us to Ruth Radke's guest house. Now, for the first time, I was introduced to what would become commonplace during our stay in New Guinea: domestic servants - "house boys" and "house girls" - as dark as the few Aborigines I had met at home, but otherwise quite different, who dressed in a semi-civilised manner and spoke a patois that sounded like broken English, but wasn't. Even their odour was distinct. (Perhaps they thought the same about us.) For Leon, it was all familiar. I could see him reverting to an earlier stage as he explained it all, but to me the foreignness was palpable.

At one point, something caught the corner of my eye, and there was the biggest spider I had ever seen, carrying a large bag on its belly. I cried out to Leon to kill it – which he did. But the whack which ended the adult's life broke the sac, and a host of tiny, baby spiders scattered hither and thither – and that first encounter with the native wildlife has remained vivid in my memory all my life.

However, our stay in Lae was brief. Pastor Wilhelm Bergmann, whom, you will remember from chapter 2, Leon had met in 1946, had returned home to Germany on furlough, and it was Leon's job to relieve him. After a short flight to Goroka, we were met by a church representative with a four-wheel-drive vehicle, and headed west. For the first time, I experienced the reality of roads macadamised by hand ie by labourers manually, painstakingly, and often crudely, covering them with large stones, followed by progressively smaller stones: rough, often narrow roads, not infrequently stripped of their gravel and rendered slippery by torrential rains.   Also, for the first time, I experienced the magnificence of the Highland scenery: rivers churning at the bottom of deep gorges, the grandeur of the Dalau Pass leading to Watabung, the luxuriant greenness, and the variegated human mosaic of native villages and gardens, and expatriate plantations.

The chief town in the Chimbu district, Kundiawa gains from its altitude of a kilometre and a half a milder and more pleasant climate than that of the sweltering coastlands, as well as a certain relief from mosquitoes. Ega (pronounced *ay*-ga) was a Lutheran station nearby, now under the supervision of Pastor Roland Brandt as *locum tenens* for Pastor Bergmann. They greeted us on arrival, introduced us to the station and its staff, and the next day hurried back to his parish at Omkalai.

Our trunks not having arrived, we had to make do, essentially, out of our suitcases. We had been assigned the downhill house of the two mission residences.   From what you have read of my childhood, you will appreciate that my standards in accommodation were not excessive. Nevertheless, I could not help noticing a few defects in this new dwelling. True, there was plenty of living space, but it was built on stilts, and shook like a baby's cradle when we walked around. Our beds were iron frames with mattresses which sagged in the middle. The interior décor was brown and white, and after lights-out there could be heard the scurrying of hundreds of tiny feet, and in the morning traces of cockroach footprints over the white sections. Nor was this the only nocturnal noise. The station, to its credit, was well furnished with vegetable gardens and citrus and banana trees. The first time we acquired a bunch of bananas, we hung them on the verandah to ripen. That night, I was awoken in alarm by a terrific din of flapping and squawking. No need to worry, said Leon; it was just a flock of flying foxes making a meal of our bananas. In time, I got used to it, but the next time we got some bananas, we found a safer storage place for them.

Our water supply for the house was from the rainwater tanks. Up on the hillside was a small stream, on which Russell Scherer had put in place a Pelton wheel to bring the water to the station, with small channels to direct the water. The wheel was connected to a generator to produce electricity for the station, so the pipe accomplished a dual purpose of water and power supply.

Although washing procedures were not markedly different from those in rural Australia at the time, they were nevertheless heavy. Clothes had to be soaked in washtubs, boiled in a copper heated by a wood fire, and wrung out by hand. At least I had the help of a native assistant. The outside toilet, on the other hand, was just a hole in the ground, which filled up with water periodically. To venture forth at night, among the toads and the snakes, could be a hair-raising experience. Leon made it his business to erect a new one.

As for the wood stove in the internal kitchen, it also had to be replaced. The firebox had burnt through into the oven itself, with the result that when I attempted to bake bread, the flames rose up right around the product. The fact that bread making was an unfamiliar activity for me did not improve the situation. At first I was determined to do without the assistance of a *haus kuk* boy, but when we moved to the Bergmanns' larger house, I had one. Those were the days when my cooking was of the archetypal new-bride's standard: bread that was heavy and burnt, and chicken soup which was so salty it was virtually inedible. ("It doesn't bother me," said Rev Brandt, who was visiting at the time. "My grandmother used to do it that way.") My mulberry jam just would not jell. I had jars of the stuff when we moved on, so I just left it behind, but Mrs Bergmann sent it on to us. (How kind of her!) Fresh meat was rare, but some of it was processed in Agee jars, and wasn't bad.

Fortunately for Leon, he was able to get down to business right away because of his knowledge of Pidgin. Also, Ega had a quarter century of experience behind it, and the local parishioners knew what was expected of them. This would be the point, therefore, to introduce a special group of workers unknown to our home churches: the evangelists. These were the pioneers and foot soldiers of the church militant: native Christians who, with their wives, planted themselves in distant, heathen villages, setting up house with minimal financial support from the church, to preach the gospel in a language and cultural context familiar to their listeners. These, rather than the white missionaries, were the true heroes of the mission field, and their portion of worldly fame has been as small as their reward in heaven will be large. Whenever a group of New Guineans was to be received into baptism, they were always asked, "Who will go to such-and-such a place?" If no-one was prepared to go, it was assumed that they were not yet ready for baptism.

The approach of Christmas forced us to improvise. A casuarina, or she-oak, could pass for a Christmas tree in the absence of conifers. Strings of popped corn and strips of aluminium foil served as decorations. The local people brought us some honey, which we heated to remove the dead bees and the wax. At this point, a certain ingenuity was called for. Americans, particularly in Hawaii, know of an ornamental plant called "palm grass". In New Guinea, it goes by the name of *pitpit*, and it is used for food. (I can provide you with recipes for it.) Leon took some small, hollow stems of the grass, threaded some cotton through them, and filled them with wax. Hey, presto! Candles. It was one of our more memorable

Christmases.

Right after Christmas, Leon set out on his first expedition into the interior. From Ega we could gaze out at the peak of Mt. Erimbari, 30 kilometres to the southeast in a direct line, at the foot of which lay Monono mission station. Bob Heuter, its pastor, had asked him to accompany him into the Bomai, south of the Wahgi River, and an officially restricted area. A reverse apartheid applied in New Guinea. Whereas, in South Africa and Kenya the natives required a permit to enter the white zones, over here permits were needed for whites to enter the most traditional native areas. The reasons were obvious. Violence was endemic in traditional society, and the local bowmen were likely to adopt a shoot-first-and-ask- questions-later attitude towards strangers. Also, experience had shown that the sort of white adventurers who sought their fortune in such out of the way places were not necessarily sterling examples of western civilisation. The clash of uncivilised savages and civilised barbarians had left an indelible stain on the history of the nineteenth century Pacific Islands, and the Australians were not going to let it be repeated on their watch. Only when government authority had been established in a previously uncontacted area would specific westerners be allowed in. Fortunately, missionaries were considered a good influence, and it did not take long to obtain a permit.

I came with Leon as far as Monono. At the end of the main road, a chair was sent down from the station for me to be carried on the last stage of the journey, and I stayed with Ruth Heuter and her children. As for Leon's adventures, nothing beats a contemporary record, so I shall quote the article he wrote at the time for his hometown newspaper.

BOMAI

On the clear morning of Dec 28, 1954 Rev. Heuter and myself left for a trip into the Bomai (South Country), South of the great Wahgi River. Nancy, the horse I rode, was a bit tired from the three-hour trip up the mountain to Monono the day before. The other horse was fresh and frisky.

We had nearly 30 carriers including evangelists and others who wanted to go just for the trip. At about nine in the morning we started and rode until noon when we stopped at a Kiap station for lunch. The Kiap is the government officer who looks over the natives and takes up their troubles in a court that he conducts. The Kiap (District Officer) whenever he comes uses the Kiap houset, and people traveling through   may also use it.

From the station, Koromane, where we ate, the Wahgi River had a fast descent.   After nearly sliding over the horses' heads going down we decided that we could do it safer walking, so we sent the horses back to Monono.

The Wahgi River gorge is similar to a little Grand Canyon. To give you an idea of the amount of descent and rise the altitude at Monono is 6500' [approx 2000 metres] and the Wahgi River about 3500' [approx 1070 metres] at our first crossing. After coming to the river the bridge was in such a bad condition that we could not cross.   The day before the natives had heard that we were coming and so they were repairing the bridge.   The wait was welcome though it was an hour long. The climb up in the late afternoon to an unknown village was difficult.   The path was narrow, steep and just plain hard work.   We climbed till late at night to get to the Kiap station of Nomane in the new land. That was a nine-hour day of traveling.

The natives in this area are quite civilized. Before going into this area many natives had talked of the cannibals and fierce men there but we encountered none that seemed so ferocious.

After a very cold night's sleep, for the altitude was higher than Monono, we fixed our breakfast and waited for the census books. It was a cold, drizzling morning and at about 10 a.m. some painted half dressed men brought the Census Books. It was found that these men came from a new area, which consisted of 1500 or more natives. Many men had two wives and several had three. The rate of men having two wives was one out of every 150 or 200. As a rule there are more men adults than women.

The next day the trip to Doulai was one in the rain and the carriers with just their lap laps on nearly froze. I was soaked to the skin with perspiration and then I took my plastic raincoat off and got soaked with cold rain. One was just about as bad as the other. Fortunately the trip was only two hours walking.

I forgot to mention that the people of Nomane brought in many chickens which we bought with little beads that they string up and make arm bands. We also bought corn, cabbage, *kaukau* (sweet potato), onions, eggs and other things with salt. Some ordinary newspaper (which they used to roll their tobacco in for a smoke) was used to buy things.

At Doulai the Rev. Brandt met us from Omkolai and spent a day with us. His mission area is right next to the Bomai area. We walked together from Doulai till the lunch hour and then parted. Rev. Brand ate lunch with us and then he walked in his circuit.

The trip to Jowai, the next village was really a rough trip. The virgin forest in that country was enchanting but it makes difficult traveling. There are many different kinds of trees that I had not seen before. Some of them are hardwood and others soft.

The people at Jowai seemed rather a dejected people. They are just about like the others that we met. They live in squat houses with their cooking fires built in the middle and no smoke stacks. The smoke just goes through the Kunai grass roof, which is what does not get into your eyes first.   The houses are dug into the ground a foot or two for warmth. The men have separate houses from the women.

The trip to Jowai from Doulai took us five hours. The altitude at Jowai is about 7500' [about 2,300 metres] and talk about cold: I just about froze there. The nice warm sleeping bag was sure appreciated. My trunks had not come at the time of this trip so all the clothes that were available had to go along and it was still necessary to borrow some to keep warm. The cold wind just blew all night long.

The house we had to sleep in was the usual kind for Kiaps. It is built on stilts and has a woven pit-pit floor. The sides are of the same woven material and the roof is Kunai grass. Sometimes the sides are doubled for warmth. There is no furniture in the house of any kind. If you want anything to sit on you take it along. We took several cots along previously used by the army and used them for our bedrolls as well as for tables and chairs.

The people of Jowai seemed the unfriendliest of all. They brought very little food but they did bring us firewood. We were going to buy some chickens there with the usual beads but we had run out of mixed beads so we mixed the yellow and blue beads which come from Italy and in the process they spilled. You should have seen the mad rush to pick up beads. Of course they put in our container what they could get. There were hundreds of beads just left lying around and the next morning all the kanakas were there picking for themselves. It was a real haying day for them.

On the trip over to Jowai I counted the flowers to see how many kinds there were and that day I counted 23 varieties. The following day there were 15 more to add to that list.

In all of the villages that we came to we gave them the Gospel and it was really thrilling to see so many people listen so attentively to the Word, which was given through translators. Every one of the villages, that is head area villages, asked for an evangelist. One also asked for a doctor. When I said head villages that I have mentioned, such as Nomane, Doulai, Jowai and Kiari. There are many smaller villages off the track from the main ones.

The trip to Kiari from Jowai was a very rough one too. There were many times in the journey that we made that there were narrow slippery wet rocks to cross where we could have fallen hundreds of feet to death quickly but the Lord was surely with us protecting us.

The village of Kiari was the same as the others as to type of people. In this area there were not many natives. Through the whole trip we found about 3700 to 3800 people who do not know Christ as their Savior.

On the way back from Kiari to Monono we descended to the Wahgi River and the bridge was completely out, so we saw the whole process of the natives building a cane or vine-bridge across a hundred foot gorge or more. It took four hours to do the work.

We did some shooting on the trip and got some birds that the carriers promptly ate, regardless of the species. The last day of the trip took us ten hours of traveling but we had the horses for part of the trip.

The trip was a hard one but it was successful. We were the first missionaries to go into the area and we ended up at the West base of Mt. Michael. The prospects for mission work in this area seem very good. How soon there will be evangelist available to go into this area we do not know since many more could be used than what are available.

The government has put certain restrictions on who can go into the new area. We had to have special permission to go in. Local evangelists can go into the area without any permit but the coastals would have to have special permits. At any rate the people are certainly ready for the Word of the Lord.

The Bomai trip ended on Jan 1 1955 when Rev. Heuter and I got back to Monono. Thank God for a good trip."

Rev. Leon Philippi

Whenever you hear of "carriers", you should put out of your mind the stereotype of Africans walking single file with great, square bundles balanced on the top of their heads. In New Guinea the men carried burdens on their shoulders, often in string bags – although string bags were (are) predominantly a feminine item. There were a few other details he could have mentioned. Whenever they came to a new village, the only people to meet them were men with bows, arrows, and axes. The women and children had all gone bush out of fear. When it came time to sleep they asked the people for accommodation, and a house would be found for them to sleep in. They would then ask to buy food, and the men would call out to the women in the bush and they would bring food in.

One night, as he was sleeping, Leon woke up and saw men with torches walking by. His first thought was that they were going to burn down the house. It was a customary treatment of to an enemy to close the outside door so a person could not get out and then light the building. However, the group departed and left them in peace.

How to describe our lifestyle at Ega? The mission houses received every year commissary from the American Lutheran Church (A.L.C.). Homes were supplied with bed linen, quilts, blankets, towels, washers, and sewing materials for the missionary wives to make clothing for themselves and their families. Also, every year the teachers, evangelists, and other native church workers received clothing from the A.L.C. women. Although the government was building up Kundiawa, there were no shops available, but we did have an airstrip, which went out over the Wahgi Gorge, thereby adding a bit of excitement to anybody flying out. For us, it was always a thrill to see the plane come in, because it would be bringing our mail and any items we had ordered. We even used to send back fruit and vegetables from Ega to Madang, for they did not grow well in the steamy lowlands.

The compound was divided into four, with the people's thoroughfare running right down the middle. There was a large church and, on the top part of the station, a trade store. A regular task was counting the takings and forwarding the money to Madang. In Australia in those days, a labourer would earn about £60 [$120] a month, but in New Guinea the minimum wage – which tended to be the standard wage – was 25/- [$2.50] a month. No, this was not exploitation. The basis of a colonial economy was cheap labour supplied with cheap food, and work was not compulsory. In the traditional villages, commerce was largely by barter, with money entering the picture only for western goods – and it went a lot farther than at home. However, the result was that the trade store takings consisted largely of small, pre-decimal coins: threepences [2½¢], sixpences [5¢], and shillings [10¢] - mostly with holes in the middle to fit on a string, and all having been passed from hand to grubby hand until the inscriptions were invisible under a layer of grime. After counting them, we washed our hands.

The station had a jeep, and a motorbike, but mostly we walked everywhere. On Sunday 24 January 1955 we walked up to Kogul in the Chuave Valley to check out some land for a school site. The scenery was fantastic, including the natural bridge over the Chimbu River, described in chapter 2. But for the first part of the journey, the roadside was covered with so much pig manure the stench almost made us sick. The result was, that later, when we had to walk up the Chimbu Valley to a church at a place called Parr, we carried handkerchiefs soaked in perfume to blot out the smell.

We did, however, use the jeep to drive to Omkalai, where Roland Brandt was pastor, driving down into the Wahgi Valley, where people were making salt, and then up a long, zigzag road to the station. The airstrip there had a gradient of one in seven, thus gaining the title of one of the steepest in the country. It was isolated. Aimee Brandt did the medical clinic work, and at the same time, like Ruth Heuter at Monono, educated her own children by correspondence. Once the kiap at Omkalai asked Leon if he could come over and fix the diesel engine that produced his electricity. Leon therefore jumped on the motorbike, and headed down the steep track from Ega to the Wahgi River crossing, only to skid over on the gravel road. He came back with the diesel engine still unseen to, and a case of gravel rash which lasted several months.

At last, the Bergmanns returned to Ega, and Leon had one last job to fulfil. The station had a jeep assigned to it, but the pastor had no idea how to drive it. Leon had to show him how. Considering the state of the roads up there, and the fact that Pastor Bergmann was already an elderly man, this was by no means a routine task.

It was now April, and time to go. We had been at Ega only half a year. Tex Mansur and his family were about to leave their station at Banz for furlough in the U.S., and we were to replace them.

A new chapter in our lives was opening in more ways than one. We were now well on our way to becoming parents. In fact, from the timetable of subsequent events, the process must have started the week before we left Australia.

Chapter 6

Banz

Leon's Story

Banz (pronounced "buns") lies to the northwest of Kundiawa, not very far, according to the map – less than fifty kilometres in a direct line. But, of course, nothing is in a direct line in that part of the world. Moreover, Kundiawa was a major government centre, for what that was worth, but Banz was a mission outpost, and to the north lay the heart of darkness. Our own journey took us down a long, winding, unpaved mountain road. Slightly more than halfway along we passed Nondugl, an experimental agricultural station where Sir Edward Hallstrom, millionaire refrigerator maker and patron of Taronga Park Zoo, had introduced sheep, cattle, pigs, goats, and various assorted crops for acclimatisation to the New Guinea Highlands, while establishing a minor zoo for animals native to the area. Somewhat beyond that, close to a vehicular bridge, we passed in sheer amazement through a cutting which had been painstakingly constructed by breaking the rocks with fire and water, over a period we could not imagine.

Tex Mansur came out to meet us and show us over the site. We were pleased to see that our accommodation would be in a wooden house with an iron roof, and plenty of room, for the Mansurs had children of their own. Nearby, on stilts, stood a guest house constructed of "bush material", with a roof thatched with kunai grass. It was to play an important role in our time there. We were introduced to the "boss boy", Kassambal, for Banz was big enough to warrant a native overseer. Tex also introduced us to the goats and pigs, and especially to a prize Tamworth boar, which he had imported for breeding purposes. "Whatever you do," he told us before going to furlough, "make sure you take care of that boar."

For transportation, we had an old jeep, and a Harley

Davidson motorbike although, still recuperating from gravel rash, I considered the latter with a jaundiced eye. Although the roads out there were rough and stony, the bridges were (mostly) presentable, being constructed of rounded logs bound together with vines, and often protected from the elements with a thatched roof.

To the north rose a mountain ridge known locally as Oiboku (where the souls of the dead were supposed to go, remember?), and far to the northeast the towering peak of Mt. Wilhelm at 4,510 metres, glittered with snow during what passed for winter in those latitudes. At Banz, nevertheless, we were still in the Wahgi Valley, and it was interesting to watch the weather patterns. In season, afternoon thunderstorms would often sweep down into and across the valley. To the north, over the mountains, heavy dark cumulus clouds would roll along, with mutterings of thunder and flashes of lightning in their van, both fascinating and daunting.I don't remember ever experiencing a dry storm there. In the interests of better radio reception, an aerial stood erect atop a very tall pole about a chain distance from the house, but whenever a storm was passing overhead, that same aerial would become the focus of St Elmo's fire - a frightening display of electric flames, spilling over into the house. So, whenever a storm was in the offing we would make sure the radio was disconnected.

It was not long after we arrived – in May, as a matter of fact – that I had occasion to climb the Oiboku. Beyond it lay the Jimi Valley, one of the dark places of the earth, which, the psalmist reminded us, are full of the habitations of cruelty (Ps. 74:20). Lest you think I exaggerate, let me quote somebody much more famous than me: Sir David Attenborough who, as a young man on an animal collecting expedition, received permission to enter a nearby region of the Jimi Valley two years after me.

About 1955, the District Commissioner told him, aircraft overflying the valley had spotted burning villages, and refugees told of wholesale massacres of women and children. A government patrol dispatched to the area ran into an ambush. The D.C. therefore went in with a patrol officer, Barry Griffin and a dozen native policemen, set up a station and, effectively, left them there. When Attenborough and his companion entered two years later, they were met by a thousand whooping, painted savages, and discovered a remarkable situation. In the previous round of bloodshed, one tribe had driven another out of its area, so Griffin's first action had been to tell the interlopers to decamp – which they did, apparently without demur. Then, in little more than a year, he had set up a station with a trading store, a miniature hospital manned by two native orderlies, and a court of justice. One lone white man, with just a dozen native police, and without bloodshed, had tamed a land of thousands of warring savages. And his reward, needless to say, has been to be completely forgotten by his compatriots. This was the face of Australian colonialism of which Australians themselves know nothing.[5]

But this was still 1955, and members of the Wangu people from the Kuno district, on the other side of the Jimi River, had come in for medical treatment and, while there, had expressed interest in having an evangelist being placed among them. We also had church workers on the far side of the range who needed a   visit, so I decided it was time to make a journey across the Jimi. You have often seen clouds clinging to the mountain tops, but you ever thought of walking inside them? Dank,   chilly, and clinging, this was the atmosphere faced by me and my dozen or so carriers, as we struggled up paths which were no more than stretches of mire and humus between the giant trees and tangled vines. In places the track was so steep we were reduced to clambering on all fours, and in other a slippery log was all that separated the walkers from knee-deep slush. And all the time, wriggling over the jungle floor, and reaching out from the underside of leaves, the ever-present

[5] David Attenborough (1959). *Zoo Quest for a Dragon*, Readers Book Club, pp 196-214

leeches sought our blood.

The poor quality of the trail was no accident; communication with the outside world was something the locals did not desire. Just beyond the top of the ridge, on the descending track of slippery red clay and stone, the way was blocked by a trellis, or arch of leaves and branches, green and freshly cut to indicate that the makers had our own party in mind. Off to the side, two posts were stuck in the ground, cut at an angle. The long, flat surface thus exposed was marked with stripes of paint several inches wide: yellow at the bottom, then blue, red, and finally black.

A sorcery gate! Some of my carriers put down their loads and refused to go on. Remonstrating with them had no effect; they were just too scared. It was not bows and arrows they feared, but the black magic of the gate, which they believed would kill them should they pass through without an effective counter-charm. And kill them it certainly would, by the power of suggestion alone – as much victims of superstition as the Aboriginal victim of a bone pointer. For those of us who were left – who were exposed enough to the word of Christ not to fear sorcery – there was nothing to be done, but to add the abandoned loads to our own and hump them to the next village, where we managed to hire new porters.

We now worked our way from 3,000 metres down to 500 metres, to the raging torrent of the Jimi. At that point, the sole access to the opposite side was a bridge of lawyer vines, for it was too swift for either fording or swimming. As described in an earlier chapter, such bridges are in the shape of a V, with one set of braided vines forming the base, and two sets above as hand rails, connected to the base by yet more vines. You had no choice but to walk gingerly on that base like an apprentice tightrope walker, trying desperately to keep its swaying under control. The entire structure must have been at least 30 metres long. It would take two or three people at one time but you did not dare walk in unison, or the bridge would be set swinging, and you could be dumped in the watery turbulence below. But we did get across safely and went to the next village.

Although we did not visit it, it is worthwhile noting that there was a village nearby inhabited almost completely by midgets, whose small size was apparently the result of inbreeding.

In the Kuno we never lacked for food. When the natives brought out their food for sale, we would share some Miti (Gospel) with them first, and then we would make our purchases. With the help of the local evangelist, we could sometimes get as many as several hundred listeners. In some cases the people responded well to us, and in other cases you could sense their negativity. One particular instance we made our talk and then went to buy the food. The people told us that they were going home with their food. They were so ashamed of the way they had treated the evangelist after asking him to come. We had to do some quick talking to keep the food we needed for the line of carriers.

And how was Theophila getting on while I was away? Well, she was busy working in the dispensary, and struggling to take care of the vegetables, flowers, cows, pigs, horses, goats, chickens, ducks, and dogs, but she was handicapped by the fact that she was female, and therefore a lower form of life in the eyes of the Melanesians. Also, she was not yet proficient in Pidgin. But she understood it only too well when the boss boy, Kassambal came over one misty morning and announced: "*Misas, pik em i-dai.*" (Missus, the pig is dead.) Which pig? The prize Tamworth boar! We think that the salt had not been properly mixed in with his food, and the greedy beast has eaten the lot.

I have just mentioned sorcery. Known in New Guinea as *sanggoma* (pronounced "*sung*-goma"), it forms such an ever-present backdrop to everyday life that tales about it can be related by anyone on intimate terms with the inhabitants. Such a person was Andrew Mild, an older missionary from Nebraska, who had lived through rather dramatic times. He had been taken prisoner by the Japanese, and then strafed by his own side, suffering a shrapnel wound that laid bare his jugular vein. Only immediate action by Dr Braun, later in charge of the Yagaum Hospital in Madang, saved his life. I shall therefore take the liberty of quoting a detailed letter he sent me on the subject, in which he uses both the Pidgin word, *sanggoma* and the coastal Graged term, *tegaum* .

SANGGOMA   SORCERY   (Tegaum)
as recorded by Andy Mild

"For this particular type of Sanggoma Sorcery the motto could well be "under on the March". The underlying motive is the eradication of an enemy or one with whom one does not have the most friendly relationship.   For those who possess this sorcery it is a great power, and for those who do not possess it, it is also a power but one to be feared, for the possessor of that power need but spread the rumor that this power will be used and all tremble with fear. We need not think that only the poor ignorant New Guinea native fears this sorcery, for it is also found in such enlightened countries as Germany, Romania and others.

Preparation

"This particular type of sanggoma sorcery is practiced by a group, not by a single individual. When the group has decided to eradicate some individual or individuals, they begin preparation at once. The period of preparation may last months or even a year due to difficulties in obtaining proper sorcery material. The most important and prime prerequisites are the body of a newborn baby. When a child is born to a woman who does not want the child, she immediately kills it and buries it. At once the uncle of the deceased child exhumes the corpse and takes it out into the jungle where he builds a small rack and places the tiny body upon it. Over the rack he places his fish traps, bows and arrows, spear, hatchets and herbs. The purpose of this is that the spirit of the child will aid him in all his daily ventures, his hunting, his fishing, his work, and warfare, also for his medicinal ventures.

"The following month is spent in smoking the tiny corpse. At the end of this period the body is so dry and hard that decay will not set in. Then this body is tied onto a small flat stone that for generations has been used for this purpose. Tiny armlets and bands for the legs are made and placed on the child. On the left wrist is fastened a particular type of wristlet that makes the corpse sacred. Now the preparation of the corpse is complete — its purpose is that it will be both the building and protecting spirit of the sorcerers.

"Further preparation consists of the following: the vine of a wild yam, a bone-like section of a tree called *Sumbinun,* and an herb known as *ngisingees* (Graged) are placed together in a clay pot. This is charred and then taken from the pot and powdered with the left ulna bone of the sorcerer's deceased uncle. This preparation is to be used as a hiding magic. Then with the ulna bone of the deceased uncle the sorcerer outlines on the ground the feet print of a cassowary, a dog, a pig, a crocodile or wallaby. From that time on his footprint will not be that of a human being but rather that of the animal of his choice.

Practice of Sorcery

"When the preparations have been completed the group starts out to obtain their end. En-route to their object the spirit of the child acts as a guide, both protecting and warning the murderers. If any individual should approach, the group is warned by the spirit of the child through the cry of a particular bird. When an individual approaches the murderous mob applies its hiding magic, (in the form of a black power previously described) to their noses. As the individual approaches they hold before their noses a leaf or a twig. If the intended victim himself is a sorcerer of another group he will see the sorcery group as individuals, but if he is not a sorcerer he will see the sorcery group only as a branch of a tree. If he is an individual who is not a sorcerer he will innocently approach the place in the path where the chief sorcerer has placed his magic herb (Ngisingees). When he sees the herb on the path he at once knows what has happened. He recognizes the sanggoma sorcery material and intense fear takes hold of him and he becomes insane. Then the sorcerer strikes the man with his knife, spear, arrow or hatchet. He falls and the natives all believe he is dead. At once the chief sorcerer instructs him to return to his village, instruct his wife to prepare an excellent meal, to eat it, and go to bed and die, and the obedient victim does so. His fellow villagers may not be aware of his condition, but the next morning he will be found dead.

"The Sanggoma do not depart immediately; they may walk through the village as friends and enjoy the gifts and hospitality of the villagers, for they have removed their magic potions and will not be recognized as sorcerers by the village. They usually depart to another village to visit friends or for the purpose of trading before the murder is discovered. On their return they will secretly go to the burial place of their victim, taking a bit of the earth, turning their hands to the side and spitting the earth out. This they do so that the spirit of their victim will not harm them.

"There are many inconsistencies in this account, but reasoning means nothing to the average native. They have seen the power of this practice and they fear it. Consequently the fear is so great that actually they are the victims of the wiles of Satan. In New Guinea the contrast between light and dark is very great. Also the contrast between the power of God and power of hell are very great. Hell's weapon, fear, God's weapon, faith and courage.

"What makes this so powerful is that the individual who has ever brought this before a court of justice has never won his case. Consequently the sorcerers do not hesitate in pointing out the fact that even the white man with all his knowledge and prowess can't defeat them or learn the source of their power."   (A. Mild.)

I can add details of my own. In the Rintebe district sorcery was also very common. If it failed in its effect, Plan B was to waylay the victim, knock him on the head, and then force slivers of bamboo under his tongue to prevent him from speaking upon regaining consciousness. Bamboo slivers were then also inserted into his rectum and under his arms to cause infection.

White magic and pagan rituals were even more common. The Banz people would kill pigs to appease the sun god, so that their boys would grow up healthy and strong. Offerings of pigs were also made to the sun to ensure good weather. On the other hand, a purely magical approach to rain making was to go into the bush to find a wild taro plant, wrap it in a banana leaf, or some other big leaf, and place it in running water. Customs such as these die hard, and formed a barrier to the spread of the Gospel. Another common excuse for not coming forward and accepting Christ was that other people in the village would ridicule them (an excuse not unknown in Australia). With the children, it would be the parents who made fun of them. On the other hand, often the parents failed to take much notice of their children's education, until the children themselves brought the Word back to them.

In the church I used to communicate in Pidgin. However, I was also forced to learn a little Kâte ("*cut*-ay"), a coastal language used by the native teachers. It was Lutheran policy to use Kâte for instruction in the Highlands, and Graged in the Madang area, but because they were totally different to any

European language, they were difficult to master.

Theophila often accompanied me in field trips closer to the station. In one of them, a new village school was opened up, and we ended up sleeping on a platform of woven bamboo on a dirt floor. It was   here that she experienced her first *mumu*, the cooking procedure traditional to most of Melanesia and the Pacific, where custom built ovens, iron pots, and pressure cookers were in short supply.   First, a pit is dug in the ground half a metre or more deep, a fire made in the bottom, and river stones piled on top. They have to be specially chosen, for some will explode on heating and turn into projectiles. The best ones are volcanic. Once the stones are sufficiently hot, masses of pork and chicken, along with taro, sweet potato, and other vegetables – all wrapped in banana leaves – are placed on top. Then more leaves are added, and the whole covered with earth. At several points, bamboo shoots have been inserted into the *mumu*, and down these water is poured onto the hot stones. Suddenly, steam in seen billowing from the bamboo, but most of it is trapped underground, in the manner of a giant, earthen pressure cooker. After one to three hours, the earth is removed, and a delicious feast is served. Such was the process at every important function.

In July, we flew down to Madang, and headed for Yagaum Hospital, which I had assisted in building so many years ago. There, on 20 July 1955, just three days after Theophila's birthday, Peter Leon Philippi, our first born, was brought into the world. I registered him with the American embassy, and Theophila registered him as an Australian. However, she has always said that she would have faced a lot fewer bureaucratic hurdles if she had been my mistress rather than my wife, for an illegitimate child automatically acquires his mother's nationality. In any case, all of our children have dual citizenship, although two now live in Australia and consider themselves Australians, and one lives in Texas, and considers himself American.

He was baptized at the church in Nagada, outside of Madang, by his father but, of course, it was a long time before he was old enough to realise that the surroundings in which he was being brought up was unusual compared to those of other white children. At least Banz could not be considered socially isolated. While we were there we witnessed the first vehicle come through from Lae *en route* to Ogelbang, and we also saw the Lae Highlands Highway being pushed through by the Dillingham Construction Company. But even before the roads were improved, there was constant movement between the various mission stations, both by automobile and by air. The guest house saw frequent occupation, by visitors from other denominations, and even by high ranking Lutheran officials from Australia, the U.S., and Germany.

One of the more memorable was a great mountain of a man, Dr Schuh, the president of the American Lutheran Church. Inevitably, he received the initiation given to just about every visitor to Australia or its territories: we offered him Vegemite. Sharing knowing glances, we watched as he made the mistake of most visitors: he spread it as thick as jam. Would you believe? He scoffed the lot without so much as a grimace!

(And how long, you may ask, did it take me, myself an American, to get accustomed to Vegemite? Well, I never have. I prefer Promite. Isn't that taking assimilation far enough?)

One couple, Gloria and Bill Meuser came to Banz and established an agricultural school. Until their home was erected, they lived in our guest house. On Sundays after church, we would have dinner together, and often the pilots and their families would join us.

Banz had its own airstrip, and the Mission Aviation Fellowship (M.A.F.) had a base right on the airstrip, whence they ferried, not only missionaries, but also food and equipment to all parts of the Highlands. Guests would also end up staying overnight if they arrived by air, and the weather prevented further flying that day. Passengers usually came and went in a Cessna, but a weekly DC 3 flight was required for the mail and cargo. By now, not only was Banz self-sufficient in fruit and vegetables (and was also growing rye, plus a thousand coffee trees), it had also become the market garden for Madang, and one of my weekly assignments was to purchase enough fruit and vegetables for the return flight.

On one occasion I had an order for fresh pork for the hospital in Madang. The day before the weekly flight, therefore, I drove up to a plantation called Kotna to collect a dressed pig. All went well until, on the way home, just before dark, I was crossing a timber bridge, when one of the wheels of the jeep suddenly slipped between two of the logs. A close inspection revealed that the cords binding the logs had either broken, or come loose. In any case, the wheel was stuck.. It was beyond the strength of one man to lift it out. There was nothing to do but leave the pig in the vehicle and hike back to the plantation, by which time it was too dark to take further action. Telephone communication, needless to say, was non-existent in that area so, while Theophila sat at home with baby Peter, frantic with worry and praying for my safety, I was left to shiver back at Kotna. It was so cold, they lent me a pair of woolen socks to keep me warm.

Come the morning, I returned with enough men to liberate the jeep. At least the cold night shouldn't have done any harm to the carcass, but now the sun was up, and a long journey to Banz lay ahead. As it was, by the time the carcass arrived at Madang, an odour of putrefaction hung about it, and was it was solemnly declared unfit for human consumption.

As for Theophila, she was by no means leading a life of carefree idleness. Peter, my son, you have no idea how much one tiny human being can add to a mother's work load, and cut into her free time. Apart from keeping you supplied with milk, and your nappy (diaper) constantly changed, she still had the normal routine of running a household. There was, for example, cooking. She worked out infinite variations on the preparation of canned meat, and discovered that fresh goat meat can be made to resemble lamb. Fortunately, in the washing department, she had assistance – and needed it. When told that there would be washing machines in New Guinea, she naïvely assumed this meant automatic machines. In fact, it meant having one of the house boys or girls standing over a galvanized tub driving a plunger up and down by hand.

As a registered nurse, Theophila took charge of the dispensary, a work she enjoyed. Once a native "doctor boy", or medical orderly was posted there, her main contribution was supervision, and advice on symptoms and treatment. However, for the first month or so she was working flat out three hours every afternoon. In a line that never ended came the wretched victims of accidents, violence, and a host of loathsome tropical diseases. Those requiring an overnight stay arrived with their families and food, and often a dog or a piglet, the latter suckling at a woman's breast like her own baby. They came in their native garb of grass skirts and *asgras*, but one day a very big man arrived with a wonderful headdress, and all sorts of charms hanging on his wrists and arms. Under the one arm he wore a braided charm that indicated he was a witchdoctor. A couple of pointed bones were also held in place by an armband. He had a fine stature, but the look in his eyes really intimidated her, and she prayed to the Lord for His protection as she treated his condition.

One night early in our stay at Banz, at about 8 o'clock, we had a native boy brought to us with two willfully inflicted tomahawk wounds on his thigh and lower leg. We were fortunate that he was not in shock, and the hemorrhage not too serious. We looked after him for the night and next morning sent him to the doctor a day's journey away for stitches.

God only knows how those poor people must have suffered for thousands of years, before the coming of modern medicine! Malaria was not so common in the Highlands, but cuts, abrasions, malnutrition, common colds, and diarrhoea were *de rigeur*, not to mention leprosy and yaws. Occasionally people would turn up with their face and nose eaten away by tertiary yaws, but thankfully, mass treatment throughout the

1950s has reduced this horror to only a few percentage points of its original prevalence. One of the long treatments she had to administer at Banz was for tropical ulcer. It required bathing with a saline solution two or three times a day, and then dusting with Iodaform powder. This had a very pertinent odour which, once smelt, is never forgotten, but it served the purpose. These ulcers sometimes were on the face, by the ear. Once we encountered one that had grown completely around the calf of the leg. We were thankful when that was healed.

Another infection was ringworm. Some people had that all over their body. A topical application of salicylic acid (i.e. aspirin) solution would take care of that, but treatment had to be persistent. (It also had an expected consequence to me, as will be explained in a later chapter.)

On one of my bush trips I found a child that had a full mouth of teeth but when brought in to the dispensary, weighed only 6 lbs [less than 3 kg]. Its swollen tummy was the result of being fed sweet potatoes instead of milk.Theophila immediately took charge, and it wasn't long before the child was putting on weight. The people quite often saw white women feeding their babies with bottles, and thought it a good way to do it, but they did not know about the cleanliness and fastidiousness that goes with bottle feeding, so quite often children died.

The circumstances were unusual when I performed my first wedding, and the only one in New Guinea. Across the Wahgi Valley stood the Swiss Brethren station of Minj, where three couples had just arrived from overseas, but not registered to perform weddings. Being requested to do the job, I set out with two visiting girls from the Madang Supply House tagging along for the experience. I drove as far as I was able, and then had to hike one and a half hours along, and several times over, the fast flowing Minj River to perform the ceremony.

An even bigger event was the traditional wedding of our boss boy, Kassambal, who lived in the village nearby.

According to custom, his wife had been chosen by his paternal uncles - not without his consent - from one of the neighboring villages, and they had lived together for more than a year, demonstrating both that his wife was a good housekeeper and worker, and that they were fertile, for they now had a baby daughter about a year old. So, strictly speaking, they were already married, but now the time had come for it to be made irrevocable with the finalisation of the bride price. (Needless to say, the "down payment" had already been made, and would need to be returned if the wedding were called off – thus creating a disincentive to a too hasty divorce.) The groom and his family approached with a great banner, for want of a better word, displaying masses of tiny shells known as *giri-giri*, huge, golden *kina* shells, great, glorious bird of paradise feathers, and Australian money, along with spades, axes, and pigs, pigs, and more pigs. Kassambal and his friends were decked in all their finery: head bands of tiny shells, lip shells, feathers, body paint, and the obligatory bows and arrows, without which no New Guinea male would feel properly dressed, any more than a European gentleman of days gone by would appear without his sword. Likewise, his wife and her female friends presented covered in grease and paint, with headgear of feathers and tree kangaroo skins, in a grand procession from her parents' village. The pigs, of course, were eaten in one gigantic mumu feast.

From this you will have gathered that, in this area, the wife came to live with her husband's family, and inheritance of land and property passed through the father's line. In the language of anthropology, marriage was virilocal and descent patrilinear. While you might find nothing unusual about that, in many parts of the country, the reverse is the case: marriage is uxorilocal (the husband joins the wife's family) and descent is matrilinear (through the mother). You must understand that, traditional Melanesia is largely a horticultural society, and although the status of women is low, they do the bulk of the agricultural work. If you are the male head of a family, it is in your interest to keep your daughters at home, even after the bride price has been paid, so that they can tend your gardens. The downside is that your sons are scattered among other families, and they are your fighting force. Therefore, the crucial issues is: whom do you fight? If the neighboring villages are your friends, and combine with you to fight the tribe in the next valley, then it is safe to have a matrilinear society. But if you tend to fight the people of the nearby villages, this will not do; you have to be patrilinear. You can see, therefore, the tragedy of the Bougainville civil war in the 1990s, when a matrilinear society divided on political lines, with the result that brothers fought brothers, and fathers fought sons. It also gives you an idea of the pattern of conflict in the Banz area.

Kassambal and bride, with child
(The groom appears to be smoking and chewing betel nut at the same time.)

In fact, the people on one side of the river once decided to use our airstrip as a battle field. The quarrel, as was often the case, was about a woman. A large war party, waving spears six foot long, tramped out onto the field like a Roman battalion. Roman soldiers used to form an armoured line, each man brandishing a short sword in his right hand, while protecting his own left and his comrade's right with a great shield. Likewise, our Melanesian warriors of the first rank defended the line with shields of hoop pine two or three centimetres thick, 60 centimetres wide and twice as high, with perhaps an axe in the free hand, while behind this barrier the archers stood waiting. What happened? Nothing. The other side failed to show up.

Meanwhile, to the west, on the other side of Nondugl, near Kerowagi, in a village called Ambang, no planting was done. They had stored up food in advance for this, the year of the *singsing*, or festival. At a place chosen for this, they constructed a long house used for kissing. It was a kind of initiation for the teenagers. Pig grease smeared over their skin, the girls wore their grass skirts woven into strings, open on the sides, and tied to the waist, to indicate their single state. The young boys were also greased all over, and wore fresh croton leaves front and back in a bark waist band. The young people would then go into this house and partners were chosen and they sang and kissed. Legs were crossed and they kissed until the chins were swollen and sore - in some cases weeping. I can't remember how long this went on. Everybody dressed up in their finery of bird of paradise feathers, flowers, bands of pretty green beetles, Christmas beetles, and *tanget* leaves, and they danced and danced until the ground shook. It also was a time for the killing of pigs, and what a big occasion this was! Over a thousand pigs went into their mumus.

Towards the end there stood the *Bollim House,* or Spirit House: a tiny hut raised off the ground on four stilts, and surrounded by a circle of pig skulls. Along came some special men wearing shoulder length wigs of human hair, and decorated with green beetles, or Christmas beetles. The faces were highly painted, and all very grand. During the dancing -

forwards, backwards and around - the wigs were taken off and placed on the *Bollim House*. People came from far and wide to view this. It was a most colourful occasion, and it will be a long time before so many bird of paradise feathers, and other decorations will be seen.

Under their arms the men also carried gourds full of lime. This was used to counteract the alkaloids in the betel leaves and nuts which, as with the people of India and southeast Asia, is chewed as a stimulant. The red saliva it produces is finally spat out, and can often be found decorating the streets and paths of New Guinea to this day.

Finally, not long before we left Banz, there was the issue of the Jimi Valley mission. I sought to return to the valley to follow up the work of the evangelist. But when we arrived at the river, we found that the inhabitants had cut the bridge down to bar our passage. Considering the amount of effort involved in constructing such a bridge, they must have been really determined not to let us pass. On the other side they stood, brandishing their weapons. "Go away!" they shouted. "Your trousers won't stop our arrows!" Just the same, word had leaked out as to what had been happening over there. A kiap had been there trying to keep the peace, but with limited success. Fighting was still going on. At one stage, a village had been organizing a big *sing-sing*, when the rain bucketed down and washed away their body paint. That was a good enough reason for another fight. Obviously, their enemies had worked magic to wreck their party! Twelve people were dead, and quite a few more wounded before it was all over. The evangelist, along with a few others who had listened to the Word, had managed to straighten out a few fights before the kiap arrived, but he admitted that while such violence was in progress, people were not interested in listening to the Gospel.

But soon it would no longer be my concern. We had been in Banz more than a year. The Mansurs were about to return from furlough and, on 7 June 1956, Dr John Kuder wrote us a letter directing us to go to Begesin, because the incumbents, Gary and Jean Reitz were leaving to work in a seminary in Sumatra.   He continued:

" The Begesins are not among the best of our people and will require of the missionary there that he be willing to try to understand them and their problems and much patience in putting up with their very evident shortcomings. However, if the missionary can learn to love the Begesin people he will find that they will respond as people do in other places too."

So, this time we would have a permanent post, and it looked like a difficult one.

Also, we were now expecting a second addition to the family.

Chapter 7
Begesin
Theophila's Story

Begesin was one place I had been dreading, because it was so isolated. You would not think so from the map, which places it not far from Madang, but it was accessible by neither wheels nor wings. From Madang the road led west to Amele [*um*-el-ee], and then to the Gogol River. And then it stopped. The stifling blanket of heat and humidity reminded us that we were no longer in the Highlands. Beyond stretched fifty kilometres of narrow, uneven, often muddy track to Begesin. Fortunately, being only three months pregnant, I was still able to ride a horse, and Peter, at not quite twelve months of age, could easily be carried.

The first stage of the journey took us through rain forest so dense and tall that the ground was in permanent twilight. In those days no timber interest had marred the virgin forest, so we marveled at the gigantic trees, the vines twisting upwards from the ground and, high in the canopy, a riot of orchids, crow's nests, staghorns, fungi, and mosses. At various points, one would discover a stream spanned by just a large tree, felled as a makeshift bridge, and negotiable only by two legs, leaving the horses to ford or swim.

The end of the day brought us to the half-way village of Yahl, where, as usual, the people offered for sale their local food. Of course, we had to do our own cooking before retiring, and Leon had to see to the horses with the native carriers, who were boarded in the village. We ourselves occupied the *haus kiap*, a resthouse for traveling government officials. In this case, we found it a simple, unfurnished bush house floored with the trunks of palm trees, known as *limbum*, nice and rounded to make sleep just that little bit more difficult. Came the morning, we were again on our way, first crossing the Yahl River, which at this time of year was a mere shallow playground for the local children. Winding through the jungle, down into valleys and over the streams, the track led us in the afternoon to the hillside where the Begesin mission station awaited us.

There stood a large, L-shaped house, with a kitchen and dining area occupying one side, and two bedrooms on the south wing. The fine screen which sealed off the bedroom wing stood as a reminder that, here in the lowlands, we would be contending for occupancy with the mosquitoes, and regular anti-malarial prophylaxis would be essential. A neat cot stood waiting for the baby, while strips of *konda*, or lawyer vine, supported the mattress of our own bed, and its legs were of flour drums. The entire building was floored with a particularly hard, termite-resistant timber known as *kwila* ["queela"], kept smooth and shiny by our two house girls rubbing it with coconut shells.

The church had   already been standing for more than twenty years, but you may be interested to known how it had been constructed, for the method was rather typical for the country. Wooden planks were produced by the time honoured method of pit-sawing, used in our own countries before the advent of power tools. The sawyer's platform lay across the top of a pit or, in this case, a high trellis. After a line had been ruled on a piece of timber, a man stood on the platform and guided a two-handled saw along the line, while his unfortunate assistant, the "underdog" stood underneath, pulling on the lower handle while endeavouring to keep the sawdust out of his eyes. Stems of pitpit, crushed and woven together, formed the walls. For the roof, the men bound together the trusses with native vines, then tied poles across the trusses twenty to twenty-five centimetres apart. To the women had been left the tiring task of collecting bundles of kunai grass. (Remember, the edges of the grass are very sharp, but their hands were hard from long manual labour.) The women then threw the bundles up to the men, who laid them thickly on the roof frame, where they provided a waterproof thatch lasting several years.

Inside the church, the congregation sat on benches of split timber. The walls were of woven pitpit, and the roof thatched with kunai grass. Over the altar hung a great triangular war shield, about a metre to the side, a sign that the weapons of war had been turned into the instruments of peace, and a reminder that we must "put on the whole armour of God" (Eph. 6:11). But no bell graced its steeple. In Melanesia, from New Guinea as far as Fiji, congregations are summoned, not by bells, but by a *garamut*: a drum hollowed out from a hardwood log almost twice as long as a man, and nearly a metre high, with a slot 10 centimetres wide on the top. When beaten with a wooden club, the sound of such an instrument can carry as much as three kilometres.

By now you will have gathered that a mission station is more than just a church and house. A farm with its associated outhouses, a dispensary, trade store, and school are all *de rigueur*. We had an evangelist school under the charge of a teacher named Butut, a fine man who performed his work faithfully. The same could be said for Zabut, assigned to teach the small children English, games and singing, while in the village across the Uyapan River, Tubaiya taught lessons in Pidgin.

As for myself, I shared the work in the dispensary with the native "doctor boy", Goil. I had two housegirls to assist in the home, and I was also responsible for instructing the local schoolgirls (and women) in Bible studies, and such skills as hygiene, cooking, laundry, and sewing. Some of them eventually acquired Singer sewing machines, and set themselves up in business in town. Now you will perhaps understand my complaint that the work of the missionary's wife is underappreciated.

We had been settled in Begesin for only a couple of weeks when I became violently ill with morning sickness. Our only communication with Madang was with an old and temperamental radio, but after 15 or 20 minutes of frustration, Leon managed to connect with his old friend, Dr Braun of Yagaum Hospital, who advised him to bring me there at once. This time, I made the two day journey on a stretcher. Peter came with us, not only because there was no-one to care for him at the station, but because he was also sick. Fortunately, he recovered a lot faster than I, and he was able to return with his dad for a fortnight of "batching".

At the end of the fortnight, not only was I ready to return home, but Leon had to return for the District Conference. It must be explained, at this point, that the Evangelical Lutheran Church of New Guinea (ELCONG) had been incorporated as a church in February that same year. That meant that it was now independent, and responsible for its own organisation. Each district had a native District President selected by his own people, as well as a white leader, the District Missionary for guidance, the ultimate aim being to help the church develop and take over responsibility from the whites – as has subsequently occurred. Each district would then hold an annual conference, organized and run mostly by local people.

This time it took place at a village near Madang called

Bilbil, noted for its production of clay pots. At a typical conference, all the various circuits would send delegates, and the local people had to supply the food - mainly taro, sweet potatoes, coconuts,   sugar cane, plus a lot of leafy plants and, of course, pigs. On one occasion, when the conference was held at Yahl, we brought along a gelding which had been particularly difficult, and he also was added to the menu. The white delegates, needless to say, had an irrational objection to eating horse, but none of the natives complained. When it came time to serve the food, they would use wooden or enamel bowls, or simply the bottom part of a palm leaf.

As the district conferences would last three or four days, a lot of preparation was in order. For a start, guest houses had to be constructed from scratch for all the delegates. Offerings were brought from each circuit, to be counted by the treasurers and put away for the work of the district and the church at large.

But I digress. By the time of the Bilbil conference, I was well, and it was time for the return journey to Begesin. This turned out to be   "quite a trip". We were driven to the usual spot for crossing the Gogol River, only to discover that the horse I was to ride had saddle sores. So a change had to be made, and I got the horse originally assigned to Leon. But after some time, he got tired of walking, and chose to ride bare back on the saddle sore horse, with Peter as company.

We came to the first village, but when, after an hour or so the first carriers also arrived, they informed us that one packhorse had dumped its cargo and returned to the Gogol River. Two of the boys went after it. Fortunately, we had brought some food with us, so we were able to eat before pushing on, taking a spell along the way to wait for the carriers to catch up.

In our minds we had tentative plans to sleep in the haus kiap at one village, but this was broken down, and the police boy's house was ready to fall down with any gust of wind, so we made a final push to Yahl for the night.   On this stretch, our other packhorse managed to have his luggage fall to the ground. The second time Leon attempted to fix it the horse became angry, dumped both packs and made a dash towards my horse and the one without a saddle. Peter – thank goodness! - was being carried by one of the girls, and was safe. Leon said that I handled my horse well. The runaway horse was caught, and after Leon managed to pacify it, he was able to lead it on to Yahl.

By the time we reached the haus kiap at Yahl we were pleased to find that our food had been divided into several bilums. (A *bilum* is a large string bag, normally used by women. They wrap the loop around their foreheads, and drape the bag, with its heavy load, down their backs – a method which must place a lot of strain on their necks.) We were therefore able to eat right away, get the sleeping bags unrolled, have a swim in the river, and go to bed. Next morning it was found that my horse had also developed saddle sores, so I had to ride bare back. Even this made me sore. At that time, you must remember, I was not as familiar with horses as Leon, and I was pregnant, so I ended up riding uphill and walking down. We were just so thankful to arrive at the end of the journey, to have some food, water, a shower and a rest.

After that, I had a normal pregnancy, but was advised to return to Madang for rest three weeks before the expected birth. Prior to that, my parents arrived from Australia to keep us company. Even that was not without a certain amount of drama. A white mare called Cement was sent down as my mother's mount. But since Cement was almost as pregnant as I was, her saddle girths were left purposely loose. Too loose, in fact. While crossing a stream (it may have been the Yahl), the saddle slipped sideways, and Mother slipped into the water.

Another time, when she was forced to answer a call of nature at night, we suddenly heard her yelling for help from the outside toilet. Racing to the spot, we flung open the door, and found her aiming a pool of torchlight onto a snake, which had placed itself between her and the door. Leon, however, had come bearing a hoe, and immediately dispatched the serpent. It was a reminder of what we would all have to face for the next two years, until indoor sewage could be provided.

Dad had to return home early, but Mum stayed until the baby was due. To be precise, she remained at the station to care for Peter while Leon and I made the trek to Madang. No doubt it was rather brave of her, considering her complete ignorance of the language, but somehow it never occurred to us that they would be exposed to any danger or problems – nor were they. As for us, although I was eight months' pregnant, it would be shank's pony all the way. There was no question of my riding a horse, or even mounting one; I was far too rotund for that. But when we finally gained the road, a vehicle took us to Nagada (*nug*-a-da), a place just north of Madang where our friends and colleagues, Ed and Esther Hartung lived. We had stayed with them before, when Peter had been born.

Leon then trudged the trail back to Peter and his mother-in-law, while I settled down to relax. But it wasn't to be. Our daughter was eager to be born. She came two weeks early – on 16th January 1957, just three days before her father's own birthday. No word of this leaked out to Begesin. The mission station possessed neither telephone nor telegraph, and while I was at the hospital, it never occurred to us to ask the radio operator to send a message. When Leon arrived at Nagada a week later, with Peter and Mum in tow, they were surprised to discover a brand new baby girl awaiting them. At the age of eleven days, she was baptized by her father, Esther Theophila, with Ed and Esther Hartung standing as godparents. You may be interested to know that the two Esthers remained in communication ever after, until the older one was taken to the Lord.

Mother flew home soon afterwards. Soon afterwards came the day on which Leon had arranged horses and carriers for our return to Begesin. Esther was carried in a *bilum*, or string bag, on the back of one of the native women, just like a New Guinean baby, and kept dry by a cape of sewn pandanus leaves, which the coastal people use as a rain coat. For the fact was, January is the height of the rainy season, and whereas Leon had arrived during fine weather, by now the monsoon had struck with all its fury. The Gogol River, knee deep when Leon had last forded it, was now a raging torrent. We remembered, too, that the last mission had lost a carrier here to a crocodile attack, but right now the danger we faced was more of drowning than being eaten. A bamboo raft was therefore acquired from the village, and each horse was taken across in turn, swimming for its life while being held by a man on the raft. At last it was our turn. Thank goodness both the children were too young to appreciate the danger! I was terrified out of my wits as we sat on the cross piece, with our feet in the water, the rain sweeping down upon us as we were poled into the swirling stream.

Looking back on it all now, I cannot understand why we did not turn back. It was not imperative that we return home that day; we could have waited. The porters, hired locally, could have been dismissed at this stage. In any case, now that we were on the far side, there was nothing to do but continue. Certainly, having got that far, we could see how Almighty God had looked after us: "Lo, I am with you always, to the close of the age" (Mat. 28:20). (A cynic might recall another proverb: that there is a special Providence who protects fools.)

Wet and weary, we eventually found ourselves at Yahl, and did our best to sleep. Come the morning, we were faced with the Yahl River, now running as furiously as the Gogol. This time there was no raft. Leon drove his horse in first, only its neck and shoulders showing above the water line. I might be able to manage that too, I thought, but what about the baby – and Peter? Halfway across, he halted, and turned to face me. The image is still etched in my mind: Leon standing there, up to his crotch in swirling water, rainwater pouring down his rain coat and sou'wester. "You can't cross here!" he shouted – a conclusion I had reached independently. His steed was mired up to its belly in silt.

Somehow or other, he managed to get the animal free, and

the villagers were helpful in finding a more suitable site for fording. In the process, however, the lead horse was set upon by a swarm of wasps whose nest had been disturbed, and no human being could stop him from bolting. It took a long time to catch up to him, and it was a very relieved party who wandered, bedraggled into Begesin.

As we were soon to discover, this was typical of the wet season. At a later date, we received 600 mm [24 inches] of rain in twenty-four hours. Boulders as large as three metres were rolled down the adjacent Uyapan River during the flood.

Even so, the Uyapan was hardly our enemy. Sometimes, when Leon was away on circuit, I would take the children and the native girls down to the river to swim and play. Otherwise, we would go picnicking upstream where the river surged through a narrow crevice, and one could even find the leaves of fossil ferns among the rocks. The girls used to love the crevice. Likewise, they also loved to play in the moonlight, dancing in circles, singing, and clapping their hands. Of course, it goes without saying that, as soon as they were old enough, our own children would join with the native children in common play. In 1957 Leon had some some steel wheels with an axle sent in from Madang and, with the use of some local timber, manufactured a small wagon which served the children, both black and white, as a plaything for many years to come. No doubt the native children continued with its use long after we left Begesin.

I cannot remember the year, but one New Year's morning, after a night of heavy rain, the girls who slept in a house close to ours – the schoolgirls, and our two house girls – came running with the announcement: *"Papa! Papa! Snek i-stap!"* (Father! Father! There's a snake present!)

Rapidly donning his clothes, Leon loaded his .22 Remington rifle and followed them to the fowl house. There lay a huge python, its belly so distended from the Moscovy duck it had swallowed, it was no longer to able to force its way back out through the wire netting. Once Leon had dispatched it, we discovered it was approximately three and a half metres long – twice the span of a man's outstretched arms. The families from the evangelists' school ask if they could have it to eat. Of course, this fitted in with a book we had recently read about Africans preparing a delicious snake meal, so here was our chance; we requested a piece for ourselves as well. However, I couldn't do a thing with it. I boiled it, I fried it, I think I even pressure cooked it, but the only result was a tough and greasy mass of vaguely fishy flavour, but quite inedible. I should have asked the evangelists' wives for advice.

Just the same, we did consume the occasional wild game. Norap, our boss boy, who managed the staff, also doubled as shoot boy, and would go off with a shotgun, to return some time later with a cassowary or a crown pigeon. The latter weighs more than three kilos, all white meat, but it is now a protected species.

The rice huller we purchased that year was emblematic of the complicated economic situation in the area. A money economy was only slowly developing. The local people needed money, not only to pay the annual ten shillings poll tax levied on every adult male, but also for the most elementary of modern consumer goods. We supplied much of the latter at our trade store but, of course, they had to get the money from somewhere, and the fact was, Begesin was so isolated that there wasn't much opportunity to earn any. Indeed, one of their main sources of income was working for us – for example, as carriers – which was all very well, but didn't actually do the church finances much good. At that time, a rice project had been started at Yahl, and many of our people had invested in it, with the result that they fell short in their contributions to the church. One can hardly blame subsistence villagers from seeking to improve their lot, but Yahl was effectively an economic rival to the church. In any case, rice was available, so we obtained a huller with steel rollers so that we could eat polished rice instead of brown rice. The idea caught on, and soon the local people were growing it themselves.

The local people used to work every second week on the rice project, until it came to an end in 1960. Realising that they badly needed further economic development, Leon got a native labour line to dig trenches for a Robusta coffee seedbed. As coffee is a forest tree, and needs shade, he planted lucinna trees among the seedlings. Nevertheless, it was a long term project. Coffee has to be several years old before it can be planted out, and it takes a few years to mature and bear fruit. But once the red berries were ripe, they would be picked and fermented for a few days, then washed and dried. After that, the beans would be hulled by machine and were then ready to be sold at market as a source of local income.

We also planted breadfruit around the boundary of the station, so that the roasted seeds became an addition to our diet. Meanwhile, the children chewed the sap like gum, and the adults would put a small ball of the gum on their *kundus* to give them the right pitch.

There were few dull moments sharing work with the "doctor boy" in the dispensary, with Leon helping out in cases of emergency – assuming he was not on circuit. For real emergencies, we could always contact Yagaum Hospital by radio. One day the students from the evangelist school were cutting grass with the *sarip*, a long handled piece of steel with a sharp edge, somewhat like a machete. The knife slipped and cut the artery on his wrist just below the thumb. The young men staunched the blood flow, and brought the lad in to get fixed. Unsure about what to do, we now began a frantic search for Dr Braun. The radio, of course, was its usual temperamental self – and all the time the poor fellow was in danger of further haemorrhage. After that, we were unable to get Dr Braun at Yagaum. We tried Port Moresby, and they finally managed to put us into contact with him. Advancing to the microphone, Dr Braun handed out instructions: first sterilize some cotton thread, then take a pair of forceps, hold on to the bottom end of the artery, and tie the thread through the artery so it cannot open up. Then apply the forceps to the top end of the artery, repeat the procedure, and then close the wound. I gave the injection to kill the pain, while Leon did the sewing. Alas! He was a handyman, not a surgeon. The lad healed up well but the tendon was cut, so he could not use his thumb. We sent him out to the hospital, where they fixed the matter up. He returned wearing a cast which, once it was finally removed, left the hand with nothing worse than a scar.

We had broken bones to deal with as well. One young girl presented with a fractured bone protruding through the flesh on the leg. We had to clean it up and pull the leg to get the bone back in place and then put a splint on the leg. Some straight forward fractured arms also turned up, and I'd tell them: "You'd better walk to the hospital".

"Oh no," would be the reply. "You fixed that person's arm and it was all right."

Then there was the lady who cut off her breast. Trouble feeding her newborn child had brought on mastitis. She came over to my dispensary, and we commenced penicillin injections. Naturally, this involved a course of continuous daily treatment. It started well, but then she failed to attend, and I made enquiries among members of her own village. "Oh," they said, "she has gone to the local witch doctor, and paid him money to kill a fowl on her behalf. Only that did not work, and the breast dried up, and she took a razor blade and cut it off." I told the people that she had better go to the Yagaum Hospital. The people concerned walked her out, and she was there for little while, but did not stay too long. She was home before it was finished healing.

We had another instance with a newborn babe had been thrown down a latrine hole by its mother, because it was illegitimate. This was a matter for the the authorities, and we notified the kiap.

Another time, a man presented with a triangular piece of skin hanging from a bleeding wound on his forehead. It turned out he had fallen from a roof while thatching. On that occasion, also, I administered the local anaesthetic while Leon did the stitching. He was gradually getting the hang of tying knots and sewing up people. However, when the necessity arose for me to sew an ear back on, Leon was on circuit, and sorely missed.

At the base of the mountain, on the far side of the Uyapan River, stands the village of Gonogol, and one day a group of people from that place carried in a young girl with a serious injury. They had been chasing pigs, and when their quarry fled into the long kunai grass, they sent a number of girls in to flush them out, while the men waited with bows and arrows. Only the big boar this girl encountered had no intention of fleeing; it turned and gored her. Needless to say, it didn't occur to them to bring her to us right away. She was left in the village for three days, by which time the wound had become septic. We kept her for treatment, and I tried to syringe the wound, but the tusk had not simply ripped the thigh, but had passed right through it, with the result that the syringing solution came out at the other end. Persistence paid off, however, and we were able to send her home alive and well. In all these things I was very aware and thankful to God for his guidance.

Certainly, our medical work opened opportunities for the spread of the gospel, but our presence was not universally appreciated – especially not by those to whom we represented competition. At first, we obtained all our water – and very good water – for both drinking and washing from a nearby spring. One day the girls came back from the spring bearing back a small stone pierced with a hole. Sorcery! It had been hung over the water to poison those who used it. Leon hung it up in front of the house, by the trade store, for all to see the contempt a Christian holds for black magic.

Another time, they brought from the forest some sticks in some vague resemblance of a human skeleton, and put them on our veranda while we were sleeping. The idea was that our bones would break and we would die or leave. That didn't work either. In Gonogol, the village across the river, they held

114

special singsings to get rid of us. When all else failed, common, simple intimidation was resorted to. While Leon was away on circuit, and I was left alone with just two small children, they would come out at night and wake me up by banging on the galvanized tubs in the laundry. How often was Leon away? I counted 126 days out of 365. And, as often as not, he would return home with a bout of malaria.

What with a sick or absent husband, a demanding baby, an energetic toddler, the women's classes, the dispensary, the trade store, banging laundry tubs, as well as the usual run-of-the-mill housework – all in an atmosphere of oppressive tropical humidity – a missionary wife ran little risk of sinking into indolence and boredom.

One thing, however: we were never left defenseless. We were well aware that our families and congregations at home were surrounding us with prayers. Indeed, Leon's Aunt Lizzie used to set aside a certain time of the night to remember us in her prayers. And, as Lord Tennyson put it, "More things are wrought by prayer then this world dreams of."

Begesin was a place where everything seemed to go slowly because we had to either walk, or ride horses. The rainy season was particularly bad, as our experience with the birth of Esther demonstrated. Often on our trips in and out we had to contend with rain, slippery trails, landslides, and fallen trees. At times we would be forced to wait two or three hours for a flooded stream to subside enough for us to ford it.

In the early days, six months might pass without our seeing another white face. For the delivery of small to medium sized items, we were reliant on air drops. Once a week a Cessna would fly over and drop our mail and meat while *en route* to the Omkalai airfield in the highlands. Sometimes on the way back they would also drop us some fresh vegetables. We were so thankful for that as we could not grow the vegetables we were used to, and we were forced to eat a lot of the local produce. When the aircraft was expected,   we would place a big white cross out in the middle of the yard for the pilot to use as a target. Once I had my watch repaired, and it was returned in the mail package, ticking along faithfully, unaffected by the airdrop. Only once or twice did the pilot misjudge, and drop the cargo in the bush, but it would always be found and brought back to us. To give credit to the Begesin people, although the coast people referred to them as uncivilised "bush kanakas", over all the years they carried our supplies, nothing ever went missing, except, once, a couple of torch batteries.

Just the same, during the monsoon, there were often times when neither aircraft nor carrier could get through. One year, six weeks passed without mail or supplies. Even my yeast ran out, and I had to produce some of my own from potatoes. (How do you do that? You chop up a small potato and lemon, boil them in a cup of water for five minutes, then remove all but a few small bits of potato, add some salt, sugar, and and half a cup of flour, and leave for twelve hours. This is a recipe handed down from antiquity, which provides a breeding substrate for yeast cells floating in the air – though it is uncertain, and sometimes captures species of yeast unsuitable for bread making.)

But there were items which could not be air dropped. Like a refrigerator. Its lack was sorely felt when we first arrived, but Conference granted us one in 1957. In due course, word came from Ivan Amman, the resident missionary at Amele, that the kerosene driven Charles Pope refrigerator had arrived at the Gogol River. At once, Leon rounded up carriers and hurried down with a roll of shillings strung together through holes in the middle. He then rode back to Begesin, only to receive word that the carriers had reached Yahl where, to put it mildly, they decided the crate was too big and heavy and the pay too small to justify their lugging it any further. Leon had to then get on his horse and ride back with some more strings of silver coins to change their minds.

The narrow uphill trail on the last stretch of the journey

was apparently really tough going for the carriers, but I shall never forget how my heart leaped for joy when I saw this long line of men bearing that huge crate around the corner of the hill, and down into the mission station. Its presence made our lives so much easier. Meat goes bad very rapidly in the tropics, but now we could have it flown in once a week, and also store the milk from our cows, and keep our vegetables fresh.

It was a pity the refrigerator contained no freezer. Once in a while we would butcher one of our surplus cattle, but although some of the meat could be preserved for a long time by pickling in brine, most of it would have to be given away as we just could not use that much meat at one time, nor did we have the facilities to keep it.

Conference also granted us a rainwater tank. Word was received that the iron would be sent to Amele, and then delivered with the goods to the Gogol River. Carriers were dispatched to the delivery place, and after deliberation the men decided that there must have been something wrong: the iron was curved! Either they thought they were doing us a favor, or perhaps because it looked difficult to carry, they set about flattening it. When the Amele missionary came down to see how things were progressing, he looked on the results with dismay. He had to collect it all and take it back to the mission store in Madang, then arrange to send out some more. This time the curved iron was delivered safely. It certainly was not an easy load to carry and the carriers were paid accordingly.

Next, Leon set about constructing the tank. First a tank stand was built. Then the curved iron had to be joined, first one, then the next, until the four were riveted and soldered together. The bottom had to go on before it was soldered. The top was put in place by bending it over the top. Leon is an expert handyman, but this one tested his skill. Five times the tank was put in place and five times it had to be taken down, until all the leaks were repaired. However, once it was all fixed there was no more carting and carrying water for the house. The stand had been made high enough for the water to flow into the taps by gravity. We could also have an indoor toilet – but that had to wait for another day.

At long last, an airstrip was put in place. After a site had been chosen and the necessary agreements with the people across from the station had been made, including payment handed over for the land and the movement of several houses on the top end, work proceeded on clearing land, and various other preparations. Drains needed to be dug and filled with stones, all without machinery. A manual lawn mower had been sent so that we could mow around the station, and later on the strip. The whole operation lasted many months, including periods when Leon was away on circuit. I had trained one of our horses to pull a scraper that could take about half a metre of soil at a time, and horses were often brought into other aspects of the job as well. Then, one day, while Leon was away, a workman came running over to tell me that one of these horses had fallen into a deep trench. I found it lying there with all four legs sticking up in the air. The labourers had to enlarge the ditch to extricate it.

A tall post was cut from a kwila tree in the forest, dragged alongside the river as far as possible – for the timber is too dense to float - then dragged up a lower bank to the airstrip, where it was put into position to hold the wind socket. In the absence of machinery, Leon's ingenuity was tested in the matter of raising it into the hole, but he finally decided on the use of three big konda (lawyer cane) ropes thirty metres or so in length. One of the ropes was then fitted to a fulcrum, and the pole hauled up, while the other two ropes guided it into position. Next, the post had to be plumbed, and the ground stamped flat to hold it. Finally, one of the men was required to clamber up the ten or twelve metre pole to remove the ropes, and hook the wind socket into its fittings. This he did in the time honoured manner of tying a short cord between his ankles and gripping the sides of the pole with the traction that only feet rendered leathery by a lifetime of barefoot locomotion can provide. Shoes just will not work.

Great excitement on the 20 May 1959 when the Super Cub made its first landing. The strip was the shortest strip at that time in New Guinea, only 252 metres, and the pilot had to do it right the first time, because the top end ran straight onto the hillside. I sent word to Leon, who was on one of his field trips, and nine days later the dedication was performed, and the locals gathered around for a major singsing. Later, the strip was extended to allow a Cessna space to land. On days when the plane was expected, we would have to radio to Madang early with a weather report, and ensure there were no pigs on the strip. But it eased our supply situation no end, allowed more goods to be imported into the trade store and, probably more importantly, allowed easy evacuation of medical casualties to hospital.

The following year we got electricity. Prior to that, nocturnal illumination was by means of a "tilley lamp", or pressure kerosene lamp which, to give it credit, produced an excellent light. However, we did have a diesel engine to operate our rice huller and power saw, and we were able to connect it to a 110 volt war surplus generator acquired from Finchhafen. Then, a electrician was sent over from the church to wire up the house, and on 29 July 1960 the power was switched on for the first time. Of course, it had its ups and downs. Both the engine and the generator were temperamental. Also, Leon got tired of going out at night in the rain to turn off the engine, so he rigged up a device whereby he could set an alarm clock, and at the appropriate time, a cord would pull a pin, drop a weight, and shut off the engine.

Bit by bit, the site was becoming more civilised. It was not before time. On 7 April that year, our third child, Timothy Christoph was born at Yagaum Hospital. On that occasion, we flew in and out by air, just as when Peter had arrived. After the drama surrounding offspring no. 2, it was almost an anticlimax.

Chapter 8

Trials of a Pastor

(Leon's Story)

When we were looking through old photographs taken in 1959, we were shocked at how gaunt and haggard I appeared. Begesin was not a healthy place and, particularly during the latter half of our stay, I was subject to multiple bouts of illness. Indeed, hindsight might suggest that the increasingly pessimistic tone of my annual reports to the church was influenced by the physical strain I was under.

But first things first: let me describe the routine of a missionary's life. You will have gathered from Theophila's account that, when I was home, a fair share of the work of maintaining the station property, farm, shop, and dispensary, along with the management of the staff, would fall to me. As such, it reflects the myriad of so-to-speak "non religious" tasks which is the lot of any pastor in an American or Australian parish.

As the weekend approached, I was faced with the task of preparing the texts for the Sunday sermons – not just my own. I used to write out the explanations of the texts in Pidgin, and then enter the church and provide the lessons to the evangelists in training. They, in turn, would visit the surrounding villages in pairs to preach the message they had just heard. Very often, as an adjunct to the lesson, they would take along a roll of illustrations of various Bible stories. Fortunately, in Butut, the teacher in charge of the evangelist school, we had a fine and upstanding helper, who performed his duties faithfully.

Of course, it also meant I had to gradually familiarise myself with the main local language, Graged. However, the fact was my parish covered seven different language zones, and that left Pidgin as the default mode of communication.

For most of my visits in the Begesin area horses served as both mounts and beasts of burden, but some of the country was too rough and steep even for them, leaving me to go on foot. At least our horses were wise to the bush and they would not knock you off with a tree in the path. I used to have archmesh hooked onto the packsaddles, so that, when evening came, all that needed to be done was for me to unhook the archmesh, bring the equipment into the shelter, and take what I wanted. Much of the cargo that we ordered from Madang in the early days came in by packsaddle, or by human muscle power, but towards the end of our time it was getting hard to obtain carriers, and we were really pleased to have the airstrip finally working by 1959.

Approximately one day in three was spent on circuit to the outlying villages for one or two weeks at a time - teaching, providing support for the evangelists, and giving Holy Communion. In the village of Faita, I also used to instruct one of the elders who wanted to learn to read and write Pidgin. I remember one afternoon, some time after I had entered a village, and my assistants had tied up my mount next to some good forage, they came up and cried out: *"Papa, hos i dai pinis."* (Father, the horse has just died.) What on earth has happened? I wondered, before discovering that the horse had perished from the bite of a snake it must have disturbed. The next thing I knew, the local people were clambering around requesting the dead horse as a supplement to their diet. It all sounded a bit risky to me, but they assured me there was no danger of the poison affecting them, so I gave the OK. After all, what else was I going to do with a dead horse? As it turned out, no-one came to harm from it. Snake poison is only deadly if it enters the bloodstream through a wound, not if it is swallowed. But it meant that I had to return home on foot, with my helper, Solomon carrying the saddle.

On such trips I always filled my rucksacks with clothing and food, along with a kerosene tin with the top cut off. To this I had attached a showerhead which could be opened up and shut off. Then, all I had to do was pull the bucket of warm water up on a rafter and have my shower. I also took along some cooking pots and a gaslight that used unleaded fuel, which provided a very good light, not to mention a fair bit of heat on cold days.

Often the local people would cook for me, and I learned to appreciate their cuisine. The leaves of the tulip tree were often added to meals, and were very rich in iron but were liable to cause diarrhoea if consumed in excess. Fig leaves, too were rich in calcium, and we were also likely to receive pitpit, corn, and pumpkin, not to mention the coastal staples of sweet potato, and a root crop known as taro. You might note the absence of meat from the list. The villagers had chickens, but pigs were a measure of wealth, and slaughtered only during festivals. But on longer trips, I always carried my .22 rifle to provide birds for the carriers' dinner. That was one reason I never had much trouble getting carriers. On one occasion, we were walking through the bush, a pig suddenly appeared in the undergrowth, and they urged me to shoot it. After that, they lived high on pork for a while, but I myself left it alone. Wild pig is much stringier than its fat domestic cousin and, unless it is cooked thoroughly, is a good source of trichinosis, a worm infection which is highly resistant to treatment.

Theophila would also fix me some fudge, as some of the walks were long and we did not stop to cook at noon. I brought along a flask full of water or coffee, and would have some fudge and a drink while on the move, and sometimes they gave me a cold taro to eat as well. Theophila also made bread, but the damp climate would often turn it mouldy before it could be eaten. At other times, I would make damper with some flour brought along for the purpose.

In the villages, the house that I was given to sleep in would have a bamboo floor, and sometimes a bamboo cot. At other times I used a lightweight aluminium cot which I brought along specially for the purpose. My retinue would be boarded with members of the congregation. Many of the houses   had a pitpit floor about two feet off the ground, which represented the sleeping area and the place where you were invited to sit and talk. Many a time, when I was sleeping in one of these houses, it would start raining and I would have to shift my bed to avoid the leaks in the roof. Sometimes the dogs and the pigs would go underneath the pitpit floor to sleep at night. Even more annoying inhabitants of the houses were fleas, lice and various assorted vermin, all carrying their own special germs, but the ones I hated the most were the bed bugs. They would get into my sleeping bag, with the result that I could not even take my bedding into the house on my return until it was first cleaned.

In the evening I would meet with the congregation, and have devotions and a talk with the elders and evangelist. They would report to me how the devotions were going and whether or not the people were attending church regularly. If there was a class being instructed for baptism or confirmation I would examine the group. Holy Communion was given three or four times a year, and anyone who wanted to partake was required to confess his or her sins to the elders beforehand. Considering the traditional Lutheran objection to regular auricular confessions, this might sound a bit strange, but you will appreciate that in an environment where heathen temptations are everywhere present, for the good of the communicants themselves it is necessary to adopt this sort of discipline.

We encountered all kinds of problems in the villages visited. There were interpesonal disputes to sort out too. Apart from the "normal", if unedifying church politics, people cannot come to the Lord's table if there is enmity between them. There were also marriage problems. Some of the men had taken two wives, and before they could receive Holy Communion they were required to settle on a specific one. However, they would still be responsible for the support of the other wives until the latter remarried. In the village of Usino, in the Ramu Valley lived the man mentioned in Chapter 2, who had seven wives, but in order to become a Christian he had to settle for one, and this was no easy decision on his part.

While at Begesin I made journeys to spread the Word

westward over the Ramu River, at all times accompanied by a group of lay elders and carriers. It would take several days to reach Usino and then Faita [*fight*-a] and the crossing of the mighty Ramu River. The local dugout canoes could hold up to ten people, but they had no outriggers like the coastal canoes, so you had to watch your balance. One man at the bow, and another in the stern, would feel for the river bottom with long poles, and push the canoe out as far as they could, and then continue the crossing with paddles. Up to a kilometre wide, and correspondingly deep, the river was a challenge in the best of times, but after floods there was always the danger of being swept downstream, or being wrecked on one of the huge trees left athwart our path.

On one occasion, it required three crossings in the canoe take the whole of our party over – which should give you an idea of the size of our group. When the crew returned after the first crossing, they reported that a great crocodile had surfaced close to the canoe, and could easily have capsized it if that had been its intention. It was not without a certain trepidation, therefore, that I joined for the second crossing, but this time we saw nothing. But when the third load made the crossing, the croc rose and circled the canoe several times. Obviously, it was reconnoitring the situation, and if there had been a fourth canoe load, it may well have been attacked. The elders and evangelist said the Lord was watching over us, and I did not doubt it.

Another time, after a trip to Faita, the church workers suggested we return by a different route. We took the canoes down the Ramu a long way, and then disembarked and started to walk. However, our guides lost their way, and we spent a half day literally beating around the bush, and I was relieved and thankful when we arrived safely at the next village. The Ramu Valley is covered with dense rainforest of gigantic trees with spreading buttress roots, and home to all kinds of vines, birds and animals. It was while we were lost that we encountered the biggest lizard I have ever seen: a monitor, or goanna, apparently as long as a man, which scuttled off into the underground on a set of surprisingly long legs.

The local people are familiar with this wildlife. Despite the obvious risks, they wade into the habitat of the crocodiles, and locate them in the water with their feet. They then truss its mouth and legs, drag it out of the water, and eventually eat it. I saw them catch one well over a metre in length by this method. Another custom is to crush a certain vine and add the sap to a stretch of still water, stunning the fish, and causing them to float to the surface. At one point, when I returned to Begesin, Theophila greeted me with the news that the Cessna had dropped us a packet of fish, and she had saved some for me as a special treat. "Well, that was very considerate of you, darling," I replied, "but the fact is, they have been feeding me fish – and lobster – all along the trail."

These trips to the Ramu Valley were always difficult. There were no old people at Faita; they had all died of malaria and, despite the use of both regular prophylaxis and a mosquito net, I never seemed to escape infection. This meant increasing my dosage of antimalarial drugs, but there were many varieties of drug, each with its own side effects, so you could not afford to take any one for very long. One caused some of the missionaries to go blind, and others affected the hearing, but if you failed to take the drugs you would not last long. A bout of amoebic dysentery likewise left me debilitated for a long time, and the former missionary was lucky enough to survive black water fever, which is usually a death sentence.

The natives' slash-and-burn agriculture had left Begesin perpetually prone to landslides. When preparing a garden, they would just cut everything down and burn it, the ashes fertilising the soil. But if it were on a steep hill, as was often the case, the heavy rains would wash away the hillside. I recall one area   west of Begesin where the whole ground for a kilometre and a half just slipped and covered a group of pig houses, killing both pigs and people.

Because the mission station was built next to the Uyapan

River,   the trees on the hillside were never allowed to be cut. To prevent slides we found one of the best things to plant was bamboo, whose roots would spread out into great clumps and hold the soil together. Besides that the bamboo was very useful in other ways. The local people split the bamboo into thin strips for bowstrings. A piece of split bamboo could serve as a fork when eating out of their pointed clay pots that were resting in the hot coals, and the women would use a sliver of bamboo to cut the umbilical cord after childbirth. Fresh cut bamboo was always sterile. Bamboo was also useful in house construction, for a small type could be collected from the bush, crushed, and woven into a wall for the house, a floor or a bed.   If the area were cold they would erect several layers of pitpit wall for insulation.

Bamboo was used all over New Guinea as a water pot or bucket. All that was needed was a large section, and once holes had been punched right through to the last partition, it could then be filed with water. In the Ramu area the women would tie five or six bamboo together, fill them all with water, and carry them off. When they made their *mumus* (cooking in the stones) they stick a few pieces of bamboo in the hole and covered it with ground, after which they would pour water through the bamboo on to the hot stones. The pipes were sealed off and the steam would do the cooking.

Bamboo is God's gift to east Asia and the Pacific Islands – and has been for a million years. All over Europe, Africa, and the Middle East, archaeologists find large numbers of crude stone tools made by our ancestors. However, there is a line known as the Movius Line, stretching from the Caspian Sea to the Bay of Bengal, east of which such tools are very rare. This was a scientific puzzle, until it was realised that the Line represents the probable western limit of bamboo in ancient times. In east Asia, in other words, pre-humans were making tools of bamboo rather than stone.

President Kuder was not wrong when he had told us that

the Begesin people would need "much patience in putting up with their very evident shortcomings." (See Chapter 6.) After half a year on the site, I was bewailing in my annual report that:

On a recent trip around a part of the circuit there was much evidence amongst some of the groups of Christian people of indifference to the Word. The people commune seldom and there is very little enthusiasm for doing any sort of work connected with spreading God's Word. How can you inspire people so they wont be indifferent?

You must understand that I was still a relatively new pastor, and expected everybody to be as enthusiastic as myself. Any pastor of a regular white congregation would be making the same complaints. When the time came for the 1958 annual report, on 22 October, I was bewailing the economic situation. My own stipend was paid by the church in America, although I seldom saw it. If we needed anything of a personal nature, we would order it, and it would be credited to our account. However, in its day to day running, the mission station relied upon its own finances, which were in competition with those of the rice project at Yahl. The collections for the year amounted to only £136/6/0½ (equivalent to $4,400 in 2020), which was not much, even for that place and time. Later, in Australia, I would find that running a parish on a shoestring is the norm, and still more evidence of God's providence.

However, I was able to admit that things were improving in the human field. There had been 137 adult baptisms, 200 infant baptisms, and 23 confirmations, with more infant baptisms expected by the end of the year. By any objective measure, the Kingdom of God was advancing. We had fifteen evangelists and eighteen teachers employed on the lonely business of circuit, and some of the teachers were effectively working as evangelists. We had two more men ordained as pastors, one local and one from Madang.

Theophila has already described our battle with sorcery,

so now let me introduce two outstanding laymen in our district. One from the Bemal area was called Dabus, a short man with white kinky hair, and balding. At one time he had been the main sorcerer for the area, and as such had had tremendous power and influence. Such a person is held in dread and high regard, for he is believed to be able to kill you with the power of sorcery, and the effect of suggestion makes that belief a self-fulfilling prophesy. In this case, Dabus heard the Gospel and his heart was changed. On becoming a Christian, he set about exposing all the methods of sorcery that he had used over the years. One I remember was folding up a *tanget* leaf and then putting in the leaf some miniature arrows, small stones or other items. Then the sorcerer would go to the sick person and, with sleight of hand, pretend he had extracted them from the patient's body as the cause of the disease. As likely as not, the patient would then get well, either because the disease had run its natural course, or by means of the placebo effect. (This sort of sleight of hand has been reported for witchdoctors all over the worlds, including some of our own "psychic healers".) Another time the sorcerer would take a lawyer vine about the size of a wooden pencil, and a meter or so in length, fold it is the middle, surreptitiously swallow it, then make a great display of pulling it out of his mouth. When harming, rather than healing was the aim, other methods would be called upon. The sorcerer would collect some spittle, discarded food, or other offal from a victim and then, based on the magical assumption that any two things once linked, will be permanently linked, perform enchantments over the item, and burn or bury it. The victim should then waste away and die, like an Australian Aborigine who has had the bone pointed at him.

When Dabus dedicated himself to Christ, he gave up all these dark practices, and the high income they used to provide. It was the same as in the days of St Paul at Ephesus:

> And a number of those who practiced magic arts
> brought their books together and burned them in the sight

of all; and they counted the value of them and found it came to fifty thousand pieces of silver. So the word of the Lord grew and prevailed mightily. (Acts 19:19-20, RSV)

In a like manner, Dabus' actions and testimony inspired his whole village to become Christian. There were many evangelists and church workers that came from that village and area because of Dabus. It was a pleasure to have him along on a circuit trip because his influence was so great.

That story has a sequel. In 2002, while relieving in the parish at Bundaberg, Queensland over Christmas, we met a Melanesian lady named Marian Hemsley, and were amazed to discover she was the great granddaughter of Dabus. She comes to church regularly and is very involved with playing golf. Since seeing her commitment to the church and the Lord, I think it has been influenced by what Dabus has done in her home village and community.

Closer to the station - in fact just a short distance away – lived Taisaip [*tie*-sipe]. He too had been a sorcerer and wrecked havoc on a lot of people, but the Lord entered his life, and he followed Him. He became very active as an elder and did many journeys with me. He also had leprosy but, as will be explained later, was eventually cured. When he was on circuit with me, and I was not quite sure what needed to be done or how to handle a situation, he could be relied upon to come forward with good advice and help. I thank God for people like Taisaip. By their faithful service and diligence, now largely forgotten upon earth, that the Kingdom has advanced in the way it has.

Again, there is nothing like contemporary documents so, instead of relying on memory, let me quote from a circular I wrote on 20 May 1958. Here it should be explained that the Melanesians had no chiefs. Therefore, the Australian administration used to appoint a native administrator, known as a *luluai*, with a second in command   called a *tultul*.

Dear Friends:

Today would you go with me on one of my trips? The first part of the trip takes us to Jal [ie Yahl] about 4 hours walk. About 1:00 pm four carriers come to carry the bedroll with air mattress, the clothing, food, the communion ware, a net bag with some coffee and the cooking utensils. At Jal one of the girls that used to be in primary school comes and builds a fire and helps with the cooking. Before having supper a swim in the river is refreshing, especially after riding the horse for that long a time.

The other day the evangelist came to me and said, "The Luluai of our village got up in church on Sunday after the service and said that no one is to give anymore collections for the work of the church. He said that the boss of the RPS (Rural Progress Society) at Jal had given these orders." So everyone listened and no collections were given.

After speaking to the boss at Jal about the matter he was very angry and called for the Tultul of that particular village to come, since the Luluai had been put in jail for perjury. The Tultul came and denied any part of the matter though the two evangelists from his village said that he had a part in the matter of not putting collections. We had a good talk about stewardship and what the mission had done for the RPS and the responsibility of the people to God. Some facts about the RPS were noted, that the business manager was from Baitabag Mission School, the woman who sews up clothes was mission taught, and the inspector from the government was also trained in the mission school. The leader of the RPS made it quite clear that he was not against the mission and had not made any such statements saying that no more collections should be put.

At our last congregation meeting here at Begesin the

two evangelists came in and said that the people had put a collection again, so evidently the conversation has borne some fruit.

The next morning the school at Jal was examined to see how the children were doing and to give them some encouragement and some advice to the teacher on methods etc. After that the horse was mounted and the 3-½ hour trip to Bemal was started.

The same day that we arrived at Bemal, in the evening we had a session with the elders of the different places that had gathered for the communion services. One of the problems that came up was about the teacher at Bemal. He is a local boy and not married. It is a policy of the mission to never put their own people in their home villages but since this boy did not have a wife yet they wanted him to stay at home to get a wife. However, the home people just don't get along with him. For some months now there has been talk of him being married to a girl from a nearby village. The relatives of the girl have been coming to the teacher and telling him that this girl wants him. He has had only one conversation with the girl and she wanted him too, he said. None of the elders were helping to make the arrangements for their marriage, so the teacher was angry. It is always the custom of the elders and parents, and uncles, to make the arrangements for the wedding or marriage. The number of pigs and cooking pots are agreed upon for the bride price. This matter came up at our meeting that evening and the teacher was not satisfied with the business so he did not take communion. On Sunday afternoon there was another meeting of the elders and the matter came up again. The local Pastor said he would go and straighten out the matter the next day. So on Monday he went to the parents of the girl who did not want her to marry outside of their village so she was given to a local boy that day. She had also said that she liked the local boy. After the teacher heard of the settlement of the marriage of the girl to a boy from her home village, he had enough and threatened to run away, and from the last report that is what has happened.

It is very difficult for the workmen of the congregation to get wives because they usually cannot pay the bride price and the elders of the congregation are not as helpful as they should be in seeing that a wife is available for the worker.

It is the time of the year to give communions again and that was the reason for going to Bemal. One hundred and forty five partook at Bemal. The communion service is at the climax of six sessions with the people beginning on Friday morning and lasting through Saturday night. That doesn't include the Sunday morning service. The idea of the six sessions is to prepare the people for communion and also to give them some Christian instructions in other phases of their lives, for instance some instruction in stewardship. There are also private confessions that are compulsory. In a way compulsory confessions are good. I feel that often at home too little thought is given to ones sins before partaking of communion. Usually three people, including elders and pastors of the congregation hear the confessions of the people. If there are any really bad cases that they are not sure of, the matter is brought up before the whole group of elders later on. The matter is either straightened or the person involved is denied communion. Quite often communion is denied to people, mainly for not attending church, or sins that it is plainly seen that they have not repented. On Sunday morning we had the communion service and seven infants were baptized.

On Sunday afternoon at Bemal we had a wedding. The largest group that I have seen married at one time. There were 25 couples in that group. The reason for such a large group was that most of the older people and many of the younger people have never been married in Church. Their names had been put down in the census books of the government as being married. A policy of marrying those people that have never been married in the Church has been established. Some of the people who were married were very old, faithful Christians.

On Monday morning after an early breakfast and packing up, the horse was mounted and the trip back to the station was begun. During the night a heavy rain fell and all the streams were flooded. When the stream near Jal was reached and a crossing was attempted the water was found to be so deep that it came very near the top of the horse. The horse had no fear so we got through successfully.

That was the trip to Bemal.

Yesterday another of our evangelists came in with a blood-curdling story. It took place at Sai. During the night a woman gave birth to a child.The woman previously had committed adultery with a man and had become pregnant. She had the child, and her friends washed the child and cleaned the mother too. It was Sunday morning. While everyone had gone to Church the woman took her child out to the toilet, twisted its neck, broke both arms and threw it down the hole. The evangelist came out of church and saw what had happened so he dug the child out of the hole washed it and examined it and he then gave the child a burial. The Luluai and Tultul have gone into Madang to straighten the matter out. The reason given for killing the child was that it was not from her husband.

In 1958 I was sick, and it shows in the pessimism of my annual report. As the above circular would indicate, there were problems with unmarried evangelists. When sent to a specific village, they were often accused of coming just to acquire a wife, and some were known to commit adultery. At the same time, I found myself fighting against the trend to polygamy. Many of the luluais had taken second wives as a matter of prestige, and were thus setting a bad example to the congregations. A new class was started in the evangelist school, with twenty-three pupils. Seeing that most of these would end up effectively as missionaries in the local villages, this might be thought a plus, but I was disappointed that not all the circuits were able to find men for the school. Then, when I returned form hospital in October to start the school, I found that the teacher had failed to show up, and several of the trainee evangelists had run off. In addition, two of the native pastors had also absconded. They took the attitude that their job was solely to do baptisms and give communions. Yet, to a certain extent, one could hardly blame them because, although man does not live by bread alone, it is rather difficult living without it. The station was short of funds because of poor contributions, and often there was simply no money to pay the pastors, evangelists and teachers. It was a vicious circle. The financial crisis was due to slackness in the congregations, and this in turn made it hard to remedy the situation. There had been a fall in baptisms, both adult and infant. To top it all, a great *singsing* was held at nearby Gonogol, at which many Christians, young and old, attended, and the festival appeared to have brought on a condition of lethargy, with people no longer going to morning and evening devotions.

In 1960 there was more of the same. Two pastors left, one because of old age, the other because his wife was unfaithful, leaving the circuits with no pastors. In addition, three areas were denied communion because they were not taking care of their churches. They had left them complete wrecks.

But now came a new development. We had been used to having lepers turn up at our dispensary. Indeed, we had about seventy on our list, although not all of them were taking their dapsone regularly. Then, in September 1959, a medical orderly arrived with several doctor boys from Yagaum, and took a government patrol into the Begesin and surrounding districts for a full survey of the incidence of leprosy. The results staggered the imagination. Five, ten, even fifteen lepers could be found in any one village. In one village there were thirty-three sufferers out of a total population of 215. The estimated incidence for the entire district was of the order of 450. It was probably the most infected district in the country.

The following year, quite unexpectedly, a large troop of people, their food and possessions borne stoically in net bags, appeared outside our station. We watched in amazement as the line continued in dribs and drabs all day, and in the afternoon, up strode a kiap and announced: "I want to use your radio transmitter. I have to get in contact with Madang. I've been sent out to round up all the lepers, and I need to talk to the hospital right now."

Anyone would think we were an agency of the government! His very presence upset everything. Everything had to be done right away, if not sooner. Just the same, I started up the temperamental machine, and while he stood waiting impatiently, his very presence adding tension to the air, finally made a connection with the Medical Department.

This was the sort of thing that gives bureaucracy a bad name. The department should have been aware of the extent of the problem as a result of the initial survey, but now they decided that the numbers were too large for them to handle. "Don't send them, or bring them here," I was told. "We have no room. You will have to talk to the Mission."

So I switched the wavelength to that of the Yagaum Mission Hospital, and eventually managed to talk to Dr Braun. Now, whether or not the poor doctor had ever been informed of the leprosy program, it was certainly the first time it was ever suggested his hospital be involved. He explained that the needs of the general population for medical treatment were almost unlimited, as a result of which – would you believe? - they did not have a separate ward with a hundred or more empty beds just sitting around for an emergency like this. In medicine, as

135

in business, you do not go out and drum up a whole new set of clientele without first providing extra facilities.

Somewhere during the process, we were interrupted by a loud explosion. Theophila had forgotten about the rice boiling on the wood stove, and the pressure cooker had blown its safety valve. A thick, glutinous mass was now distributed all over the kitchen. She never used the pressure cooker for that purpose again.

So, while Theophila and her girls were left to clean up the mess in the kitchen, the kiap, his medical officer, and I were left to clean up the mess left by the bureaucracy. Here was the poor kiap, with a battalion of patients just sitting around on our grounds with nowhere to go. They could, if it came to the crunch, be boarded temporarily in the local villages at the right price. (After all, what difference did a hundred or more sick people make in a place like that?) In the long term, however, a separate leper colony would have to be established. Begesin station appeared to have surplus land; could it go there? I can't say I was enthused about the matter, but those poor people had to have somewhere to stay. The ultimate decision would remain with the church hierarchy and the government, but I was not going to fight against it.

Dr Braun organized it so that we received funding for the building of the lazaret, along with funds for the purchase of local food, plus rice which, now that the airstrip was in place, could be flown in from Madang. Our boss boy, Norap supervised the construction of the buildings, the methods used being much the same as those described for the church, except that the floor was of rounded timber with bamboo matting.

But all this, including the necessary red tape, took time. The first inpatients did not arrive until just after Christmas 1960. We watched in awe as people with large, pigmented skin lesions over faces and limbs started coming in. Some were missing pieces of their ears, others, more pathetically, with missing fingers, or had clawed hands, or hobbled along on deformed and crippled feet. Dr Russell, the colony's chief leprologist, arrived to confirm the diagnosis. He also taught me how to do the suturing and tie the various kinds of knots for the biopsies. (Fortunately, leprous skin feels no pain.)

Thus began our mission to the lepers, and we were able to witness to the people of the area who had hitherto refused the services of an evangelist, and were hostile to the gospel. The patients were quite content, all things being considered, since they were living much as they did in their own villages. Although the Government supplied their food, they also had their own gardens, to give them something to do. The Government sent in dapsone tablets, and at one stage we had a nurse and a doctor boy to administer both the medication and the provision of food and day to day running of the leprosarium. At the end of every month, Theophila was required to complete, and send to the government, forms on the number of patients and the progress of treatment. By the end of our stay in Begesin a year later, we had 126 inpatients, with a total of more than 300 known lepers receiving treatment. The deformities wreaked by the disease could not be fixed, but the disease itself could be eliminated from the system, and 245 were known to have been cured by them. And, by the grace of God, this included the faithful Taisaip.

On a personal level, those last few years were very turbulent for us. I seemed to be always sick. Apart from the regular bouts of malaria from the Ramu Valley, and the amoebic dysentery, I came down with hepatitis, or yellow jaundice. The hospital doctor prescribed three months of rest at home, but because I could hardly sleep, he gave me chlorate hydrate. It worked only too well; I acquired an addiction to it, and took a whole year to overcome it. But at least the jaundice disappeared, although my capacity for work was much reduced. Then I had to attend Dr Braun for an operation on a hernia. After that, I acquired a strangulated haemorrhoid the size of a pigeon egg, which necessitated another visit to hospital. Then the hernia broke out again, and another operation was in order.

I had some sort of systemic infection which was preventing it from healing, but did not know what it could be. It was quite horrifying when the truth was finally revealed.

1961 also saw an epidemic of whooping cough sweep through the area, and carry off several of the local children. We gave injections to a large number of the children brought into our baby clinic and, of course, to our own children. Later in the year, a Government medical orderly came around to vaccinate most of the remaining children.

In the meantime, Peter had reached school age, but we could not face sending him to the missionary boarding school in Wau when he was only five years old. Instead, Theophila chose to use a correspondence course to educate him at home, a demanding task she had never faced before, while all the time, keeping an eye on Timothy, who was now a normal toddler, and into everything. And the following year, Esther would start school.

But relief was at hand. Missionaries are entitled to a year's furlough every seven years, and ours was coming up in November. Our personal possessions were airlifted to Madang for storage, so that Rev. Oscar Fuhlbohm and his wife, Eunice could take over. The sorcerers who had worked so hard to get rid of us would now have to deal with them.

Chapter 9
Out, Damned Spot!

(Leon's Story)

Furlough got off to a bad start. I was in hospital at Yagaum. The day came, however, for my discharge, and our flight to Brisbane. Theophila's Uncle Ossie Wallent opened his house to us, and I settled down to have a quiet nervous breakdown. A doctor provided me with some sedatives, I lay down in a bed beneath a row of Albert Namatjira originals – for Ossie had worked in the Red Centre - and after three days I was more or less back to normal. Eventually, however, it was time to move off to Sydney to spent Christmas with Theophila's parents, who provided us with a home away from home in the shape of a caravan nestling in their back yard. At night it was a bit of a tight fit, what with three small children in addition to two adults, and shortly afterwards, we moved to a missionary flat in Ashfield. The children at least found the whole experience a great holiday. Up to now, they had been unaware that, outside of their tropical jungle, another world existed, where everyone was as pale as themselves.

But furlough is not just a twelve month holiday. Rest and recreation plays a part, of course (heaven only knows we got little enough in New Guinea!), but a missionary is also called upon to do deputation work: to travel around the country with slides and artifacts, drumming up support for the mission field. Theophila's sister, Rosie, had married into a car dealership family, so we purchased one of their vehicles and hit the road. In January, I showed slides in Canberra and Melbourne, after which we made a full deputation tour of the Eyre Peninsula, thus introducing me to the type of country where Theophila had grown up, while introducing the natives to the situation in New Guinea. On the return journey, we sold the car back.

The last week of February found us back in Sydney, and I

was starting to get concerned about an inflamed area on my left leg, not far above the ankle. "It looks like you've sprained it," said the doctor. "I'll put a mustard plaster on it, and it should be all right."

But when I returned for the plaster to be removed, there was a great, red lesion where the plaster had been. "Don't worry about it," he said. "That is not unusual. It should go down soon." But it didn't.

It was too late to argue, however, for we were due to sail on 6 March aboard the cruise ship, *Oriana*. The second part of our furlough would be in the United States, and I looked forward to doing with my relatives what we had done with Theophila's in Australia. We would start with my brother Ernest, who was now a pastor in Boulder, Colorado, and then proceed to Muscatine, Iowa, where my parents now resided. But we all know what Burns said about the best laid plans of mice and men. More to the point is the one made by St. Thomas à Kempis: "Man proposes, but God disposes."

That wretched spot wasn't healing. Also, I was noticing a swelling in my left elbow, about as thick as a lead pencil, where the ulnar nerve should be. So, as the leisurely voyage moved into its second week, a terrible suspicion began to dawn on me. On 15 March, therefore, just three days out of Vancouver, I went into the bathroom ensuite of our cabin and thrust a pin into the red lesion. There was no pain – no sensation at all. Now there could be no doubt; I had leprosy.

Leprosy! The very word is like a hard slap against the face. It is like receiving a diagnosis of cancer, or dementia. Leprosy! Unclean! The living dead: spectres with rotting flesh clad in filthy rags, ringing bells with their clawlike, rotting hands. No – I got a grip on myself – it wasn't as bad as all that. I knew it could be cured. But still, it was not something you can expect the rest of society to understand. Mention it, and you will be treated – well, like a leper. They might have renamed it Hansen's disease, but it was still the disease which dare not speak its name.

At least now I knew why my hernia operation failed to heal. Leprosy weakens the body's resistance. But where, and how, did I catch it? Probably not last year, with the setting up of the leprosarium. Leprosy has a much longer incubation period than that. It could have been any time, anywhere in New Guinea. Lepers, I had encountered many, but never, as far as I could remember, had any intimate contact with them. Or did I? Flash forward to 2001. We were now in Australia, and were visiting Doug and Elvera Kohn, and reminiscing about our joint experiences on the building team. Doug had some carvings made by our former cookboy in 1947, and he happened to mention: "Oh, you remember Along, our cookboy in Madang with the Maahs? Well, he had leprosy. You might have caught it from him."

But right now, we had more immediate problems. Like, where could we stay while I sought treatment? Would Ernie and his wife still be prepared to board us? They had children to consider as well. In fact, would I be let loose at all? It wasn't so long ago that lepers were kept in strict isolation, unclean, not even allowed to vote. And what about Theophila? Needless to say, she was devastated by the news. Now, with three small children in tow, she faced the prospect of having her husband placed in indefinite quarantine in a strange country. She had never been to America before, knew nobody there, and knew little about the place except that they drove on the "wrong" side of the road, had paper money which all looked the same, and called nappies "diapers".

Once we were off the ship at Vancouver, I put in a trunk call to Boulder, Colorado and dropped the bombshell on Ernie. His reaction is something I shall leave to your imagination. But I explained that Hansen's disease comes in two varieties: tuberculoid and lepromatous. The former is very poorly infectious, and I was pretty certain that was what I had. When we joined him, three days later, he arranged for me to attend a local clinic, where a doctor examined both the dermatitis and my ulnar nerve. Needless to say, this was a condition he was hardly familiar with. "There are three things it could be," he told me. "One of them is leprosy."

Then he added, "It's a notifiable disease. If the diagnosis is confirmed, I will have to report it, and you will be quarantined here."

"That's out of the question," I replied. "Next week, I'm supposed to be in Muscatine, Iowa with my parents." Then I added, "I will have to see a doctor there."

"Well, if you promise to seek medical attention," he said, "I won't report it. But you'd better get it seen to."

We had only five days with Ernest and Ann before catching the train to Iowa. My parents and I had aged nearly eight years since we had last set eyes on each other, and now they had a set of grandchildren they were meeting for the first time. Dad was now retired from the farm, and was supplementing his income as a part time security officer at a bank. Lois was very disappointed when I rebuffed her attempt to give me a hug. It was only afterwards that I could explain why I was afraid to touch her. And the children were wondering why their grandmother was sterilising the crockery and pots and pans with boiling water.

He had also arranged an appointment for me the next day with Dr Radcliffe in Iowa City. When I walked into his surgery and announced that I had leprosy, he was not impressed. As the leading dermatologist in the area, he was not used to having his patients self-diagnose with obscure foreign diseases. But I got him to understand that I had seen a lot more cases of Hansen's disease in my few years on the job than he had seen in a lifetime. He told me to come back in a week's time. When I did, he took a biopsy, to be forwarded to the national leprosarium at Carville, Louisiana.

Meanwhile, my parents had turned their home over to us, while they established themselves in a nearby street with relatives. Peter and Esther, and to a lesser extent, Timothy discovered the exciting new sport of riding cardboard boxes down the stairs of the first house they had ever seen which possessed a basement. For that matter, Theophila discovered it too; watching the children, she wondered what it would be like, and tried it herself. We listened to my parents sing in the choir during the beautiful Lenten services at Zion Church, and watched the barge traffic on the nearby Mississippi River.

In due course, the biopsy results came back positive for tuberculoid leprosy. Quarantine was not required, but on 23 April, the day after Easter, I entered Iowa City Hospital for a month's treatment. This became an adventure in itself for, not being confined to bed, and not being infectious, I was given an honorary chaplaincy. At one point, I came across a Negro patient exhibiting all the signs of severe consternation, for he had been scheduled for open heart surgery. Even now, this would be regarded as major surgery; in 1962 it was really state of the art, and it wouldn't have been performed on anyone who had much of a chance of survival without it. Just as I was leaving the ward, a man in uniform grabbed me by the elbow and demanded, "What are you doing talking to that guy?"

Well! I was familiar with racial prejudice in my home country, but I thought this was a bit over the top. However, I explained quietly that I was an honorary chaplain, going about my duties.

At this he softened. "Well," he said, "you ought to know that he's doing life for murder, and I'm his guard."

To cut a long story short, I came back the next day, and found him ready to receive the Word. How much it sank in is something only God can say, for I never saw him again. But the message is clear: God puts you in places you do not wish to be because He has work for you which only you can do.

Later on, Dr Radcliffe came and explained that Iowa City Hospital was a teaching hospital with students from all over the world, most of whom had never had the chance to meet a real, honest-to-goodness leper, and would I would willing to put myself on display for their benefit? It seemed a reasonable enough request. Slides had been taken of my lesions, and the doctor explained all the implications to them. Afterwards, a number of students came to talk with me privately, and I was able to provide a Christian witness to them.

Sometime after that, I was introduced to a female medical student from Thailand, Aree Sakarin by name. Their experience with me had alerted the staff to the possibilities of a skin problem with which she was afflicted and – lo and behold! - it also turned out to be leprosy. She just went to pieces, for in her country lepers are complete outcasts. I gave her some counseling her and, like the convict, never saw her again – although I did correspond with her for a couple of years. Then, in 1969, out of the blue, we received a letter thanking us for our help. She had been cured after a year of treatment, and was now a lecturer at a university in Bangkok. As I said, God puts you where you don't want to be because other people need you there.

I left the hospital stabilised on the medicine Dapsone, otherwise known as DDS, or di-amino-diphenyl sulphone). On return to New Guinea, I came under treatment from Dr Russel, the Mandated Territory's chief leprologist, and continued the medication until 27 June 1966. In 1971, tests revealed that I was clear of the disease. My only physical reminder is a patch of skin above the left ankle, indistinguishable from the rest of the skin, which is impervious to pain or touch.

Leprosy is still a problem in New Guinea, where there were 385 new cases detected in 2006, compared to five in Australia, where it affects mostly Aborigines and migrants. I myself worked in Maryborough, Queensland in the late 1970s, and I know for a fact that it existed there – something which would have caused unwarranted alarm among the population if the news had leaked out. However, the World Health Organization is hoping to wipe out leprosy, as it once eliminated smallpox, so it is possible that we will soon see the last of this terrible scourge.

These days, anyone finding himself in a similar plight to mine, would receive the following information, gleaned from more than forty years of medical experience:

Hansen's disease is not the same as the leprosy of the Bible. What the latter might have been is still a matter of debate. Most likely it was a collection of diseases which no longer exist in that form, for the simple reason that the practice of exclusion and quarantine was successful.

Hansen's disease does not produce "bad flesh", causing it to rot and fall off. What it does is destroy the sensory nerves of the affected areas, mostly in the extremities, where the body temperature is lower. The deformities associated with the disease are the result of injuries incurred because the victims feel no pain, coupled with the poor level of hygiene and high levels of secondary infections prevalent in areas where the disease is common.

The exact mode of transmission is unknown, but is suspected to be by means of saliva droplets. It has a very low level of infectiousness. Indeed, most people appear to have a natural immunity to it. This is no doubt a result of natural selection, because the disease ravaged Europe during the thousand years of the Middle Ages, and was restricted by the quarantine principles of its Biblical namesake. Nevertheless, 5% of spouses and 30% of children living with the victims are likely to catch it, so transmission must still be taken seriously.

It is eminently treatable. In fact, for many people it is self limiting without treatment.

But I digress. From the middle of the year, I was essentially back to my old self again, and ready to go ahead with deputation work. For the children, it was one long holiday; they certainly didn't go to school. In July we took a two week motoring holiday eastward, accompanied by Lois, staying with relatives and friends in Indiana, Ohio, Pennsylvania, Washington, D.C., and back through Iowa, doing deputation work most evenings. We visited the Amana colonies in Iowa, which German speaking Pietists had set up in the nineteenth century not unlike those of the Mennonites and Amish. At Waterloo, Iowa Peter and Esther came out with model farm equipment as mementos of their visit to the John Deere factory, while our visit to the Washington Monument was made memorable by two year old Tim divesting himself of his clothes, on the assumption that the Reflecting Pool was intended as a vast swimming pool.

Washington D.C. was also the site of one last manifestation of my New Guinea legacy. I took an aspirin tablet for a headache – and suddenly my throat swelled up. An urgent dosage of an antihistamine was required just to allow me to breathe freely. Only when the emergency had subsided was I able to reflect on the background. As explained in an earlier chapter, *grile* – better known in English as ringworm – is endemic to New Guinea. Often one would encounter unfortunate sufferers whose entire bodies were more or less covered with the scaly skin lesions - which also inspire its alternate name: *pukpuk*, or crocodile. At that time, the usual treatment was the topical application of salicyclic acid which, as every schoolboy knows, is the chemical name for aspirin. Now I was allergic to this normally harmless painkiller. I have never used it since.

After that, we headed westward into my old stamping grounds of Nebraska, and then westward, showing slides and giving sermons on New Guinea all the way. In every town, we were welcomed into the homes of the local congregation, who all regarded the visit of the missionary family as a special occasion. I never ate so much rich food in my life, when often enough I would have been satisfied with just a bowl of soup.

On 3 November we caught ship at San Francisco, for the return voyage to Australia. I remember in particular sitting at a table next to the captain's wife, who was sounding off about the Australian customs and quarantine service.

"It's an absolute disgrace," she pontificated. "They have no idea what they're doing. They'll let anybody in. In fact," she added, "you could be sitting right next to a leper, and not even know it."

I kept my mouth shut.

Chapter 10
Bena Bena

(Leon's Story)

I needed that furlough. Despite the continued need for medication, when we returned to New Guinea on the second last day of the year, I was no longer worn and haggard, but was ready to face another seven years in our adopted country. Unlike the situation in our home countries, where the congregation pays the pastor's stipend, and has a choice in whom they get, on the mission field, you were simply appointed from above. And, in hindsight, one has to have respect for our bishop, Dr Kuder, for his uncanny ability to move pastors around like chess pieces, always ensuring that every square was covered. Before we even left Australia, I had received a letter from him directing us to a new station. This time, there would be no returning to the steamy lowlands; it was back to the Highlands for us – to Rintebe, just outside the major city of Goroka.

Here, at an altitude of more than a kilometre and a half, we found ourselves in a balmy climate, where home-style vegetables thrived, and bullocks were brought out at regular intervals to mow the air strip, and to plough the fields for sweet potatoes. Here, the Rev. Ken Theile and his wife, Juanita had made their home, and shared it with their two adopted native children, with whom our own children learned to play in a plastic swimming pool.

But this was only to be an interlude on our part, for I came with further instructions from Dr Kuder. As I advanced in my career, more and more was expected of me. My first two postings had been as a locum, then I had received a station of my own; now my orders were to set up a new station from scratch, in the Bena Bena[6] district. There, in the densely populated grasslands of the Goroka Valley, dwelt the 15,000 members of the   sixty-five Bena Bena tribes, each further subdivided into several clans and sub-clans. Between one and three villages formed the patrimony of the clan, each with its men's hut, where the initiated males spent the night, their wives and children dwelt in separate huts of their own. Originally, the clan formed the nucleus of social life, and the focus of individual loyalty. Exogamous the clans might be – meaning that they were required to seek wives from other clans – but every clan was potentially in enmity with every other clan. In the days before the Australians brought a semblance of law and order, the villages stood, stoutly palisaded, on easily defended ridges. Come the morning, armed with bows, spears, and axes, the men would accompany their womenfolk to the gardens, stand watch over them, and escort them back to the safety of the palisade in the afternoon. (They didn't do any work themselves, but at least they guarded the women.) Into this milieu I was delivered, in order to first, locate a suitable site and, second, to negotiate its purchase and clear the purchase with the authorities.

But first things first, and that was our children's education. Peter was now seven, going on eight, and had already missed a year's schooling in America. The obvious solutions were for Theophila to continue his correspondence course of home schooling, for which she was ill-prepared, or to send him back to the home country – perhaps for years on end. All the missionaries faced the same problem, and for this reason the Katharine Lehman School had been founded at Wau [pronounced "wow"]. It also served as the centre for the missionaries' annual conference in January, providing a welcome relief in the Highlands for those posted to the lowlands. Teachers and ancillary staff were there to look after the children's education and bodily welfare and, with few exceptions, they did their very best. But it was still a boarding

---

[6] Pronounced with a short "e" ie "benna benna"

school. It meant putting a child of seven and a half, to the angst of separation from his parents, the regimentation of an alien environment, and the stand over tactics and bullying of the older boys. Peter's years at Wau were not happy ones, and it is only recently that we really came to appreciate just how much pain was involved for both him and us. But it was the best of a bad situation.

As for Esther, Theophila was able to home school her for the next two years, using a correspondence course.

The establishment of the mission station required more than a year. In the meantime, there were pastoral duties to attend to, the first being to do the circuits, and familiarise the disparate congregations with their new pastor. In attendance came various elders, plus a thin, grey haired gentleman with an upright, regal bearing: the assistant pastor, Sigayong. He was the salt of the earth, always ready to share the Word wherever and whenever it was wanted and needed. His daughter, Lugele eventually became our house maid and nanny, with the children becoming as devoted to her as she was to them. Esther still talks about her to this day.

A few years later, Kitingnuc arrived on the scene as a second assistant pastor. More jovial than Sigayong, he shared the latter's enthusiasm for the gospel, and the outreach to those who did not know it. God had been good in providing me with right hand men, and I could not have asked for more useful or devoted helpers – except, perhaps, for those left behind in Begesin.

Both men hailed from the Kâte people of the Morobe district, which is centred on Finschhafen and Lae. For complex reasons, the Lutheran Church had early in the piece decided to cultivate this language as the medium of teaching and evangelism. Attempting to introduce it to the Highlands, however, was not successful. The Bena people rather liked their own language and, besides, Pidgin had already won the battle for *lingua franca* status by its use by the Administration.

Essentially, therefore, this left the church as the sole standard bearer for Kâte. Be that as it may, it was the only language for which we had a more-or-less complete translation of the Bible, and the *Miti Binang*, or Bible study course produced on the coast, was written in Kâte. The evangelists were thus forced to serve as translators when giving instruction. While I was there, the situation was improved by the publication of the New Testament in Pidgin. Also, a team from the Summer Institute of Linguistics (SIL) was involved in producing a Bible translation into Bena.

With this background, I made my first inspection on February 21/22, 1963, hiking for four hours from Rintebe down into the valley, wading across the Bena Bena River and into a realm of sharp kunai grass and death adders, and then climbing another ridge to the village of Hofagayufa. Not far away stood a Seventh Day Adventist mission, but conditions in Hofagayufa were primitive, with access to drinking water only from a spring a quarter of an hour's walk down the side of the hill. There we met Forogai, who had received just three years of schooling as a child, and then a little training as an evangelist before being sent off as Christ's front line soldier at Hofagayufa. Not surprisingly, he wasn't holding the fort very well. He had personal problems of his own. His son had put aside his wife, and was taking another, and two of his daughters had married locally, but without the payment of any bride price. It was disappointing to discover that there was no Miti Binang class in progress at the time, no morning and afternoon devotions, and no-one due for confirmation. Those who had been confirmed were no longer attending church. This, then, was the situation I was going to have to rectify once the mission at Bena Bena had been established.

On the other hand, I was able to inspect the village school, where seven boys and seven girls, ranging widely in age, were under the instruction of a teacher called Pewefa, working in rather primitive conditions. That the children were writing on slates was of no significance; that was standard practice in

Australia at the time, but some of them had to hold them on their laps, because the desks, crude as they were, were outnumbered by the pupils. At least their arithmetic was presentable, and they were reading fairly well from a fifth grade reader in the Bena language, courtesy of the SIL translator at Rintebe. Nevertheless, I failed to be impressed by their level of biblical knowledge, and it was of even   greater concern that many of the government schools had no religious instruction at all.

My first real circuit commenced on 27 February. On this, and subsequent circuits, you must visualize me arriving with a small retinue of elders, and one of the assistant pastors, carrying food and other paraphernalia, anti-malarial tablets for myself, and a small box for medicines for any of the sick in the villages. No *garamut* summoned the congregation; that was a coastal custom. Instead, a large conch shell – also imported from the coast – would serve as a makeshift trumpet, after which we had a wait on our hands, for time is a less pressing consideration in that part of the world. In the end, however, the pastor and his flock would make contact, a service would be held, and local issues discussed. At night fall, I would be shown to the *haus kiap* or, in its absence, one of the villagers' homes – which were quite different from those on the coast. Up here, the walls were made of either pitpit or split casuarinas boughs, but they were only a few feet high, for the huts were dug in the ground for warmth. You had to kneel down to get inside. The roof had a good pitch, and a fire was built on the ground for cooking and warmth, with the smoke seeping up through the grass roof. This had the advantage that the smoke tended to preserve the roof, even if it had the reverse effect on the inhabitants' lungs. Bows, arrows, and spears were hung up near the roof. Some of those which were given us as mementos were just black from the soot. And I absolutely insisted that no pigs or dogs be present under the sleeping platform while I was resting on top.

Honesty, however, requires that I mention that the worst

accommodation I received – and that was in our last year in New Guinea – was something like one that the first of the Three Little Pigs had constructed. It was just a round hut of kunai grass, without any door; you just had to force your way in through the grass. Admittedly, it did not leak, but the ground was soaked, and the toilet facilities consisted of just a sheet of plastic such as was used for drying coffee.

But I digress. A long, tiresome, hot walk of one and a quarter hours, up hill, down dale, and through streams led from Hofagayufa to Kapokamarigi where, in June 1962 Sinekafa, the evangelist had started a Miti Binang class of thirty seven. Considering that he had had only one year's training at Raipinka, and was forced to teach in the local language, Mumujkagaba (fortunately, his own native language) he hadn't done too badly. He had found eleven Christians in the village on his arrival, and now he had a class of twelve men, five boys, and twenty women undertaking instruction for baptism – although I discovered that their biblical knowledge was still limited. Then they presented me with an odd assortment of gifts: one pound in cash, a chicken, a tin of fish, rice, biscuits, a plate of kaukau (sweet potato), and an arrow.

That afternoon, we took another two hour hike to Getunuc, where the evangelist, Quhacnuc had been in residence since 1949. He had done a whole four years' study at Raipinka and, again, he used Mumujkagaba as a means of instruction. This time the congregation presented me with an even more heterogeneous set of gifts: ten pounds in cash, and six arrows, along with onions, peas, tomatoes, corn, and a live rooster. Also, the earth moved for us – literally. We had an earthquake. They were not uncommon in the area.

One thing that bothered me was that Quhacnuc had kept no record of those who attended instruction. The next morning we examined the thirty five members of the Binang class and, discovered, disappointingly, that they really did not know much of the basics. One of the questions which came up was: what do you do if the women come but not the men (a not uncommon situation in our own countries)? Do we chase them away? No, I replied, just keep working.

The walk to Korefegu took another two hours. The evangelist, Asonipac had had three years' instruction at Raipinka, and the teacher, Hejafa one and a half. Hejafa had started work in 1961, but the people did not support the school, so essentially nothing got done. But there was a Binang class of fifty, which both I and the native pastor examined. Here too, gifts were provided: sugar cane, a bilum containing money, one pound, three arrows, two pounds of sugar, tomatoes, a packet of biscuits, a bilum full of flour, pitpit, and a sugar cane plant for cultivation. Running my eye over them, the penny dropped. These were similar to the gifts provided as a bride price. *They were buying their new missionary.*

As it turned out, this happened in every village I entered for the first time. It was a touching display of recognition and affection for the first missionary assigned specifically to them. You can take it as read for the rest of this account, for it would be tedious to list everything placed in my hands.

The following day, 1st March, we had morning devotions, and I baptized two children. Then we walked to Sakanuga, an hour and three quarters away, mostly uphill. The evangelist, Nananepec had had two years' of schooling at Rintebe, but his assistant, Wanoc was illiterate.

On 2nd March we headed off to Kategu, another ninety minutes' walk away, where the situation was not good. Suwie, the evangelist had had three years' training, but his two assistants were illiterate. There had been no Binang class for three months, and the congregation consisted mostly of elderly women. Because the Christians themselves had ceased worshiping, there was no outreach to the heathen. But they did give us another pile of gifts similar to those received at the other villages.

Another two and a half hours, this time along a vehicular road, led me to Getarabo, by which time my feet were blistered. There were three evangelists, of whom two were illiterate, and one was inactive, although his wife was taking the Miti Binang class. We spent the next day there, and I took the Sunday service, with a former teacher and evangelist named Meopa translating. At 5 pm they had devotions.

I also heard an account of how two white men had come from Goroka and asked to preach. The congregation thought this was a good idea. They came again the following Sunday, but this time the people said: "This is not the Word of God!" In fact, the visitors were Jehovah's Witnesses. They told them not to come back, otherwise "Your trousers will not stop our arrows." I had to smile. It might have been a rather drastic response, but it was good to see that, despite the real problems in the church, they were able to distinguish good theology from bad.

On 4 March we hiked for two hours and ten minutes to the village of Napamogona, where the gospel appeared to be going strong. The elders, Itarabo and Kakmefa held regular Sunday services, and morning and evening devotions. Nailed to the inner wall of the church was a painted carving of a snake, nearly four meters long, to remind the congregation of the devil and his works. This time, I let Sigayong take the service.

Another twenty minutes away was the village of Kenimaro, where I gave devotions, but the congregation was small. They offered us a meal of bread and onions, with sugary tea, and provided us with the usual collection of gifts.

We then walked for half an hour to Mehewage, and stayed the night. The pastor there was having problems of a material nature; he had been given no ground to make a garden, and the village pigs had killed his goats. We discussed the problem with the congregation, but they came up with no solution. The teacher, Bose also had problems. He had no pupils. I made a note to have him reassigned to Bena Bena if pupils couldn't be found.

Next stop: Arufa, sixty-five minutes' walk away. Here things were very bad. There were hardly any inhabitants around, and those that we found told us that the rest had scattered, looking for food, for they were in the grip of drought.

Final stop for the day: Kaiyufa, two hours away, up a very steep hill. We discussed matters with the three resident evangelists and three elders, who were holding both morning and evening devotions, but there were only four pupils in the Binang class. They were treating the pastor at Mehewaga as their local mentor for baptism classes. .

On 6 March we went to Safanaga, twenty minutes' walk away. There was no evangelist, and no Binang class. The elders used to conduct morning and evening devotions, as well as the Sunday service, but on alternate Sundays they would attend the service at Mehewaga. The heathen said that the Christians were all dying, and so they decided there was no point in becoming Christians.

Fifty minutes further on, we came to Kokinaga, where the illiterate evangelist, Nimise had gathered together a congregation of ten men, ten married women, and fifteen widows and spinsters. It was there that I was presented with a wicked-looking, and very unusual arrow. The unfletched shaft was of cane, thinner than my little finger, and 91 cm, or three feet, long. But attached to the shaft by tightly wound strips of bamboo and cane, in the most intricate of workmanship, were three prongs, 30 cm, or   one foot long, spreading three or four centimeters apart at the tips.   Each of these prongs bore thirty circular notches – effectively, thirty barbs. The account they gave of its use was just as unusual. Apparently, if a man had stolen another man's wife, the village would be treated to public duel between the cuckold and the adulterer.   Standing a few steps apart, they would aim to shoot each other in the thigh with these vicious missiles. The barbed points of the arrow would be bound loosely, but if they met their mark, they would splay apart, making their removal from the flesh almost impossible. Often infection would set it, even leading to death. I was told about one man who had been rendered permanently lame in this manner. Even worse, one man had died as a result of such a wound inflicted by the brother of one of the evangelists, possibly sparking a vicious cycle of revenge and blood feud.

We visited three more villages that day: Keninaga, Mohoweto2, and Mohoweto1, inspecting the state of the church in each instance, and receiving the obligatory presents in return. As the people of Mohoweto 1 did not want us to spend the night there, we hiked back to Bena Bena.

And there, ladies and gentlemen, you have a picture of how a field missionary spent his time in the 1960s. I shall not burden you with an account of my second circuit a month later, covering a second set of villages. Sufficient it is to say that it was much the same as the first. You will, however, have noticed a number of points.

Firstly, a missionary in those days ran little risk of running to fat due to a sedentary lifestyle. Nor was it a career recommended for anybody with flat feet, sore knees, or objections to frequent replacement of shoes.

Secondly, there were the gifts. This was not the usual "passing around the plate". Under normal circumstances, a collection, mostly in cash, would be taken up at every service, just as it is with us, and then set aside to be brought by representatives of each congregation to the regular circuit conference. But, in this case, as on my second circuit the following month, they went out of their way to make me feel welcome with their gifts. At the end of the first circuit, I came away with:

• money, to a total of eighty-nine pounds;
• nine bilums, or string bags;
• forty-five arrows; and
• food: nine live chickens, ten gifts of biscuits, two loaves of bread, two eggs, flour, approximately nine pounds [four kg] of sugar, two pounds of tinned butter, twelve tins of fish, two tins of baby food, two of milk, and a tin each of meat, pineapple, coffee, and cocoa, plus fresh onions, peas, tomatoes, rice, corn, pitpit, sweet potato, and sugar cane (one to eat, and one to plant).

With respect to the money, this was nothing to be sneezed at. It would go a long way in New Guinea, and the people had obviously spent a long time saving it up. Initially, I explained to them that I myself was paid by the church, but would be pleased to hand over their donation to the church administration. "No, no!" they said, "this is for *you!*" There was no choice but to accept it in the spirit in which it was given. But, ultimately, it went into the general coffer.

As far as the food went, there was no other option but to eat it. Bilums, of course, were always useful, but it was far from obvious what I was expected to do with the arrows. I can only assume they were chosen as gifts because of their traditional presence in the bride price. I used to take around a few for "show and tell" when giving talks on missions in the home countries. Over the years, most of them were given away, but some I retained well into retirement. Most of those are now in the possession of Esther and her husband. I still have a few at home. Since the average reader will be unfamiliar with such items, I shall treat you to a short description.

First, there is a bow, constructed from a single piece of *limbum* palm, 62 inches or 158 cm long, and as thick as one's thumb in the centre, now blackened by cooking smoke from being stored in the rooftop of a hut. Its string is a strip of bamboo. The arrows average around four feet [122 cm] in length, the shaft generally of cane, with a wooden tip occupying at least a quarter of the total length. Unlike arrows throughout the rest of the world, they are unfletched ie they have no feathers attached to the end to ensure accuracy. On the other hand, extremely intricate workmanship is a feature of the wooden points, considering that, by and large, the only instruments used to carve them were knives of bamboo or stone. Even greater skill has been displayed in binding the heads to the shaft. Invariably it has been executed with very thin strips of bamboo, and even finer orchid stems, wrapped as tightly around the join as skin around flesh. Most likely they were applied wet, and allowed to shrink into place on drying.

I have already described the three-pronged anti-adulterer arrow. I also brought back a much plainer version, whose triple prongs measure only 11 cm, and were designed solely for killing birds or fish. For slaughtering a chicken or piglet, the New Guineans first transfix it with an arrow. The one I had was shorter than the others – only 41½ inches [105 cm] long, with a simple wooden head 14½ inches [37 cm] long, more or less cylindrical, and pointed at the end. On the other hand, the heads of the pig-hunting arrows consist of a piece of bamboo as broad, flat, and pointed as a dagger.

However, it is when it comes to killing people that the artisan's workmanship reaches its apogee. The heads of these arrows represent approximately thirty percent of the length, and are surmounted by a conical guard next to the shaft, to prevent further penetration into the body of the victim. But what holds the viewer's attention are several rows of wicked-looking barbs along the whole length of the arrowhead. In the highly ornate arrows used as bride price payment, the guard and the barbs are painted red, and often the space between the barbs is adorned with black and white orchid stems.

The simplest of such arrowheads is triangular in cross section, with a long series of small barbs. Somewhat more complex is another arrowhead, also triangular in cross section, bearing a double row of thirty barbs, all painted red. But these barbs are shallow. If the arrow pierced an enemy in a non-vital spot, it could probably be extracted without pulling out too much of the flesh. The final three, however, are truly diabolical, and the only possible way to remove the embedded head would be to push it all the way through the affected limb, then cut it off at the base. Even then, the wound would be horrific. One has a double row of six barbs, each 6 to 8 cm long; a second is adorned with a three rows of six barbs, only slightly shorter. But the *pièce de résistance* is a beautifully designed item bearing not two, not three, but four rows of four barbs, each 7 to 9 cm in length, and lying flat like a porcupine's quills, ready to skewer the victim's flesh at the first attempt to draw it backwards. It was obviously designed for a bride price, and I like to think its purpose was wholly decorative, and was never really intended to be used in combat – at least not among Christians! Nevertheless, it is only fair to mention that I knew an evangelist called Rasowe who managed to cope reasonably well with fragments of five arrows in his body.

Finally, there was a spear, 161 cm, or over five feet, long, tapered at the end, without any sharp tip. It was designed for use by a woman assisting her husband in battle, and was presented to Theophila at a village called Sigerehe shortly before we left on our second furlough.

The third thing to note about the circuit was the spiritual state of the congregations. Some were thriving but, by and large, it was an uphill battle. There were times when I wondered what was the point of going on. We had a paradoxical situation: on every side, all I could see were problems, problems, and more problems yet, by any realistic measure, there was a church growth which any pastor in our home countries would envy. But I had never pastored a "normal" congregation. This was a heathen country. It is a common aspersion that we "no longer" live in a Christian country, but the people who make it are short on both history and geography. They are unaware of how slack Christendom was in the past, and the sort of perversity which goes on outside its borders.

Jesus taught his followers to be the yeast of society, with the result that Christianity now permeates every cranny of Western society, to the extent that it goes unnoticed, like the sunshine. Much of its imagery, morality, and presuppositions is adopted unconsciously even by its enemies, having been absorbed at second hand from the culture around them. It is the fixed standard from which the rest of society deviates. The alternative is usually to believe less, seldom to believe otherwise. Outside of Christendom, however, it is the values of heathenism which hold sway, and the battle is to pry them out the minds of the new converts – and those of their children and grandchildren – and prevent them from sinking back in.

Consequently, in our own countries, a pastor presiding over a dwindling congregation is like a farmer watching his crop wither in a drought – a drought he knows will inevitably end. In a place like New Guinea, on the other hand, every congregation is a precious garden planted in a wilderness where the native vegetation, pests, climate, even the soil itself, are against it. Almost certainly the missionaries who brought our own people to Christ well over a thousand years ago, felt just as frustrated. But they persevered, and they triumphed. And so, as it turned out, did we.

While all this was going on, the search for a mission site continued. Eventually, with the help of the elders and assistant pastors, I settled on a plot of about twenty acres in the Hofagayufa area – a   stretch of cleared ground covered with sharp-edged kunai grass, with a slight upward slant from the main road, and not a tree in sight. It had been purchased from the Hofagayufa people by a Mr. H. Buyers, and the church arranged to purchase it from him. But it was not until 12 November 1963 that the transaction received official approval.

Of course, there was no road leading to the site so, using a tractor and plough from Rintebe, we prepared a side track from the main road. A ditch blocked our path, full of mud and soggy weeds, so I constructed a culvert from sections of 44-gallon drums, and had the staff pack the space with stones hauled from the Bena River. With the access road completed, and much of the kunai hacked away with machetes, the first building to be erected was a small wooden hut for the workmen, which would later serve as our laundry. They were also provided with an outside toilet. I noticed, however, that the builders were laying down the floors in Australian manner, with the nails clearly visible. That caused me to immediately step in and teach them the American system of invisible nailing ie of driving the nails through the groove of the tongue and groove joint, so that it could not be seen from above. In

January 1964, work began on our own accommodation: a prefabricated building of aluminium, about twenty-five feet, or seven and a half metres, square, which was always intended to be temporary. On 26 January, the bridge over the Bena River was washed away again, meaning that all communication with Rintebe now had to be across the ford. Our house was not completed, but we could not wait; a new couple were moving into Rintebe as teachers, and we had to move out. On 13 February we arrived with four truckloads of furniture and equipment.

That first night in the new house, our mattresses were spread out all over the floor. Theophila woke up to hear a wheezing sound next to her head, for a mother cat had brought all her family along to settle next to her pillow. Eventually, the mattresses were raised up on beds supported by old flour drums. One morning, Theophila found the cat curled up on Timothy's bunk and, worst of all, in the process of labour. "This is no good," she thought, and immediately heaved kitty up by the scruff of her neck, and flung her off the front stairs where, to everyone's horror, out fell all the kittens: one, two, three. Another time, the kittens decided to rest on the back tyre of the land rover. The first we knew about it was when I pressed the acceleration, and headed off to Goroka, and the kittens all scattered like sparks from a fire. I tell you, the cats in that place had at least nine lives each!

But I digress. The house was still incomplete. A small section was added for the kitchen. We had an indoor flush toilet with a septic tank outside. Our gas stove was still sitting at Goroka, waiting for a regulator. Most of our water came from a rain water tank, but I also found a spring outside our property. With the use of an old petrol pump, a pipe, a hose, and a bit of ingenuity, I was therefore able to provide the property with extra water for the toilet, washing, and so forth, while also assisting the villagers with their water supply.

As the sun rose in the morning, the aluminium house would creak and groan as it expanded with the heat. Come the evening, it would creak and groan again as it cooled. That house had the normal amount of insulation expected for a tin shed, but if you like sweltering on summer days, and shivering on winter nights, you would have enjoyed being our guest. Likewise, it you consider the gentle pitter-patter of rain on the eaves boring and mundane, you would have found the combination of our galvanized iron roof and the two metres of annual rainfall an exciting change. Nevertheless, despite these obvious advantages, whenever allocations of financial resources were discussed, I seldom failed to raise the point that the house was meant to be temporary. It was another two years before we even got hot water.

Bit by bit, the station developed. The kunai steppe was finally cleared. With the aid of the Rintebe tractor, I ploughed the land inside the fence to serve as gardens for the school boys. Theophila remembers me returning to the house one day with scarcely more than my eyes visible in the dust. An oval was surveyed, and casuarinas trees planted all around. Up went bush materials to construct a Bible school, to be served by a native teacher. Likewise, quite early in the piece, a small booth was raised for Theophila to use as a dispensary, and in no time at all, she was presented with a long line of patients suffering from minor injuries, diarrhoea, leprosy, sore eyes, scabies, and head lice.

You will notice that, in contrast to Begesin, the list of buildings does not include a church. My Sunday practice was to take the Land Rover as far as possible by road, then proceed on foot to one of the nearby villages, a different one each week, and conduct the service. By turning up unannounced, I would get see the congregation in its normal state. After the service, either the congregation would provide lunch, or the family would go off for a picnic on our own. In the evenings, I would conduct another service at home, this time in English.

Every Thursday and Fridays, the elders and I would hold meetings in three separate areas of the circuit. Usually it would take each evangelist at least a day to reach the designated point, and at least another to walk home, so you will get some idea of the effort put in by these unsung foot soldiers of Christ. In any case, it provided us all with an opportunity to discuss the problems of each village, but the main purpose was to go over the lessons the evangelists were to give the following Sunday. You might suppose the illiteracy of many of the evangelists would create difficulties, but they were not as great as you would think. Old Rasowe of Upegu (the one with the five broken arrows in his body) could read not a single word, but it did not appear to dampen the long term impact of his message. In later years, his son became an English speaking pastor. We "civilized" people have substituted wheels for feet, and note paper and computers for memory, for so long that we have forgotten what both feet and memory are capable of. Preliterate societies have learned to cultivate the memory. In New Guinea, details of land ownership, family obligations, and enmities, are committed indelibly to memory as a matter of course. In many parts of the world, tribal history and religious lore are taught by rote, and the listeners are expected to retain them word perfect. In such a manner, for example, were the traditions of Genesis and Exodus handed down, long before they were put onto paper. And in a like manner, our evangelists did their work.

But it was still necessary for me to take to the circuit every month or so. Sometimes, member of the family could tag along. Peter, for example, just ten days off his eighth birthday, had accompanied me on my visit to the village of Masagu, and was sleeping in the hut when, about 7 o'clock in the evening, a shout rang out. Up stepped a man with one arm, and announced that a stranger had come to "make poison" ie inflict sorcery, on the people of Masagu, but that his (the one armed man's) brother had shot him with an arrow. The brother was now said to be following his victim in the dark, but by 8.25 he still hadn't returned, so I wrote in my notes: "I can't figure these people out. Sure don't seem to have much of Christ in their lives here." Came the morning, and the story had changed. Yes, they had seen a "poison man", but he hadn't been shot - not, I suppose, for want of trying. Just another day in the life of a New Guinea missionary!

But no, I wouldn't have been surprised if the stranger had been planning "poison". Magic, both black and white, was a constant backdrop to life in New Guinea (and still is!). Just nine days before, in a place called Gitunuc, a large community ritual had taken place. A tight fitting fence of kunai grass had been erected around a small tree or castor bean plant. The villagers then filled the space with leaves, and covered them with food which had been cooked on hot stones. After that, they chewed ginger and salt, spat it on the food, and then ate the food. The purpose was to induce labour in a woman whose pregnancy was overdue. How it was supposed to work was far from clear. Perhaps even they themselves did not know. It may have been developed slowly over many generations, until the original reason had been overlaid and forgotten.

Likewise, in a village close to the Bena Bridge lived a man called Yanamisahoba, who made a substantial income in chickens and pigs by claiming to make rain. Rumour had it that the white man at the local school also paid him a pound for the service. The procedure was to insert ginger and tree sap into a banana stalk, and then place the stalk in a stream. It seems simple enough, but presumably it also involved some conjuration, or else anybody could do it. We never tried it ourselves.

Not even Christians were exempt. In one village, when the evangelist fell sick, the people called in a local witchdoctor, who proceeded to blow smoke over him, in an effort to drive out evil spirits. In another village, in another year, the evangelist was treated at Goroka Hospital, but was still sick on his return, so a witchdoctor came and gave him a brew of some sort of leaves, mixed with cooked pork. As the treatment happened to coincide with his recovery, it was not easy to argue against a connection, but I told him that he continued to listen to talk about sorcery, the talk itself would make him sick.

In another village, I discovered that a certain Christian had passed away two months before. Even Christians have to die, but the local people were up in arms – literally! - in the belief that members of two nearby villages had performed "poison" on him. At 10.45 in the morning I was presented with an angry mob wielding bows and arrows, and calming them down took the best of my abilities. No matter how common death might be, it is seldom assumed to be natural. In yet another village, it was explained to me that they used to shoot arrows into a plank whenever someone died to determine who was responsible, but they assured me that the ritual was no longer practiced. But they also assured me that the people of another village were accusing *them* of sorcery, and it would not be worth their lives to visit them.

In a village named Kenbenkuhia, something even more sinister was in progress. A haunting fear of *sanggoma* (sorcery) hung over the village. Throughout the world, the belief exists of sorcerers who can change themselves into animals – usually fierce animals. Europe, of course, has its werewolf traditions, but the lack of such dangerous creatures in New Guinea has not put a dampener on such superstitions. Here, they feared that the people of Dumpu and Safi, four days' walk away, could turn themselves into birds such as hornbills or cockatoos, and in such form kill their enemies. The Samiri people also feared the sorcerers of the Ramu region, who claimed to change into cassowaries, the largest animals in the country. The sorcerers would not kill or eat such a bird, because it is their totem, but when the Samiri people saw one, they would run and hide.

At one point in 1964, matters took a very serious turn in two villages near Rintebe. The evangelist's house in Sigeya caught on fire. It was no accident; the door was locked from the outside, and they could not get out. Fortunately, walls of woven pitpit are far from sturdy. The evangelist and his family chopped their way out, and escaped with their lives, but with all their meager belongings destroyed. The poor man also lost his brother through sickness that same year, so he went into mourning for many months, neglecting his work. The pastor then went on furlough. Then, with spiritual guidance in abeyance, all hell broke loose. Someone in the village of Namalo bought a pig from Sigeya, and it died. Then a man died at Sigeya, followed by one of their own pigs. Obviously this was the Namalo revenge for the loss of the first pig. Next a Namalo man passed away. Sorcery! Bristling with bows and arrows, the Sigeyas trooped up to the hill overlooking Namalo. Separated by the Bena River, the two sides began yelling invective. The Namalos called out to them to come to the village, and they would "straighten out" the issue, but the Sigeyas would have nothing to do with it. The resultant mêlée ended with nine people in hospital, three with very serious wounds. Fear spread through the various congregations. But after a couple of months, the Namalos, who had now resumed church attendance, made a feast for the dead man, and presented some of the food to the Sigeyas. Before then, the Sigeyas had made an alliance with the village of Fefaro, and had organized a singsing ready to fight the Namalos, but now they too held a mourning feast, and gave food to the Namalos, and it was finally "straightened out".

Such then, is the terrible burden which the Prince of Darkness lays on his subjects. But times were changing. On 23 July 1963, I came back to Motoweto 2, and found the chief sorcerer, Sumue busy preparing a feast for the village, for he was planning to cut his hair, and make a break with the old heathen customs.

Apart from witchcraft, New Guinea threw up issues which seldom arise in our home countries. On was the presence of a leper in one of the congregations. It was decided to provide him with a separate cup for Holy Communion.

On my second visit to Mohoweto 2, when I examined the Miti Binang class, one of the women had to stay outside, and recite the Bible stories which she could hear through the woven bamboo wall. She was having her period, which meant that she was unable to mix with the rest of society. Probably neither she nor the congregation regarded this as a problem. A girl's first period is a big thing in the culture, for it marks a transition into womanhood. Four years later, we had a girl called Fuketna working as a *haus meri,* or maid. One day, the people from Mehewage came in and told a string of lies to Bose, our teacher, who translated the talk to Theophila. It turned out she had had her first period the previous day, so they took her to her home village of Kokinaga, there to confine for two weeks in a special hut with minimal food and water. Once it was over, they had a big pig feast (naturally), and she came back to work, wearing a *purpur,* or grass skirt. However, while working in the house the girls wore western clothing: a top with a yoke, and then a gathered skirt.

Then there were the fights. In a village called Kerenago, the evangelist was involved in an altercation with another over a pig in his garden. This also had to be "straightened out", and eventually they shook hands, and each gave five shillings to the elder. Five months later, in the same village, there was another argument about another pig in another garden. Holy Communion could not be given until this was settled, either, on the basis of Matt. 5:23-24: "If you are offering your gift at the altar, and there remember that your brother has something against you, leave your gift there before the altar and go; first be reconciled with your brother, and then come and offer your gift."

These, of course, were matters which would normally be handled by the local (native) clergy, and came to my attention only when I was on circuit. Marriage guidance was also as much a feature of missionary life as it is for clergy at home. In one village, four hours was spent talking with a man who was not living with his wife. It became more serious when it was not just a member of the congregation, but a representative of the church who was involved. One evangelist got angry with his wife when she failed to bring in the coffee. (That was, the coffee crop, not a simple cup of the beverage.) He beat her. He beat her a second time when she got caught in the rain with the baby. The third time he beat her was when she called him *"nos no gut"* (a generalized insult), and this time he used a stick. Of course, for the time and place, this was hardly exceptional. In Melanesia in general, and the Bena Bena district in particular, women are regarded as a lower form of life, and to the Bena men, bullying them was a sign of manliness. However, it was definitely not considered appropriate for a follower of Christ, let alone a spiritual leader, and the church leaders informed him that if it happened again, he would be *out*!

And all the time, in the background, one sensed a lurking shadow: that of the false prophet, Yali. Congregations in our home countries are usually impervious to false teachings from outside. It is the unchurched who tend to be picked off by the cultists. But in the jungle which is New Guinea, the stragglers of the flock are more numerous, and more vulnerable.

Throughout the whole of the Third World, the impact of Christianity and modernism upon traditional societies have sparked thousands of what are known as new religious movements and, in Melanesia, they take the form of cargo cults. They spring up like weeds, and mutate like viruses. But in their hundred and one manifestations, certain features remain constant. They pose the question: how is it that the white man has so many material possessions ("cargo") without doing anything obviously resembling work? And the answer is: because they have somehow intercepted the cargo from the gods and the ancestors, which was meant for the black man. Indeed, during World War II, one of them, the New Britain cultist, Batari had proof – proof! - that the white men were stealing cargo intended for him. He had seen troops unload and carry away a box marked, "BATTERIES".

The Rai Coast, north west of Madang, had been a breeding ground for cargo cultists for decades, but none more influential than Yali Singina. A war hero, he had been brought to Australia three times, but his interpretation of what he saw was somewhat off centre. For instance, when he discovered New Guinean idols in the Queensland Museum, he concluded that the gods were held prisoner there, that the visitors were worshipers, and the white coated attendants priests. So that was why the New Guineans were missing out on their blessings! After the war, he set up the Rai Coast Rehabilitation Scheme, with the support of the administration, who saw him only as an outstanding war hero, and a supporter of the colonial system, who was even preaching against cargo cults. Thus, when he was summoned to Port Moresby in 1947, he fully expected the Australians to give him access to the secret of "cargo". Naturally, he returned disappointed and disillusioned, and so commenced a cult of his own.

From 1950 to 1955 he was in prison for deprivation of liberty and incitement to rape. By the time we arrived on the scene in Begesin, however, he was out, and tales of his alleged supernatural powers were infiltrating into our area. Imagine my chagrin, therefore, to discover that his influence had now spread into the Highlands, under the name of the *lo-bos* ("law boss") movement! Following my circuits, I started to hear stories of his agents' activities on the fringes of my parish: of meetings held on Tuesdays (Yali's birthday), of baptisms designed to cancel the effects of Christian baptism, of weekly sermons in which Yali's messages, or alleged messages from the spirit world, were imparted. There was nothing else I could do but to strengthen the congregations and their teachers with the truth of the gospel, and pray that the word of God would prevail. Nevertheless, although Yali is said to have renounced cargo cultism just before he died in 1975, his movement is still going strong. No doubt it, and other cargo cults, will continue until civilization fully catches up with Papua New Guinea. But we in the Western world shouldn't be smug. Think of all the utopian promises made by the various secular ideologies of our own time!

In the meantime, something had to be done about Esther's education. In 1965, by which time she was eight years old, we enrolled her in the public school at Goroka. But there was still the problem of getting her there. Fortunately, the Lattimores, who owned a local coffee plantation, agreed to take her with their own three boys when they transported the milk to Goroka, provided she met them at the corner store. In Goroka, Lorna and Louise Vogt managed a guest house, and agreed to Esther staying there Monday to Friday. But after a while, it was discontinued, as Esther found this unsettling.

The following year, Tim and Peter joined her. (There was, after all, not much point in keeping Peter at Wau while there was a school close to home.[7]) Apparently, Timothy was a bit of a chatterbox, and one day he got his mouth taped shut. It was the only way his teacher could get him to stop talking! (Not much has changed in that regard in the last forty-five years.) Needless to say, the transport system was far from satisfactory. The children had a long walk to the corner store, often hitching rides on native vehicles to get there, and often returning home late. They also regularly turned up at school after the arithmetic lessons had been completed.

The mysteries and randomness of human fertility are a reminder that we are not in charge of our lives. In a period of five years, our first three children had arrived, and now, after a lapse of another five years, we found ourselves expecting again. Theophila's labour began on Monday 7 June 1965, about seven a.m., when her membranes broke in Goroka Hospital. As for me, I had my work to do, and children to take care of. If this sounds odd to the current generation, you should understand that the custom has arisen only in the last few decades of the

---

[7] Maybe. Leon's 1965 notes that Esther started school on 26 January, and that Peter was picked up at Wau on 28 November, at the end of term. His diary for 1966 says: "1 Feb.   Timothy's first day at school in Goroka. 2 Feb.   Peter to school in Goroka." However, neither he nor Esther, nor their parents, could remember his ever being at Goroka. Perhaps "Peter" was a misprint for "Esther". However, Peter assured me he was at home, at not boarding at Wau, during the crisis in July (which see), but he could not say what school he was attending. Perhaps he was on holidays. MS

father being present at the birth. Indeed, in our time, a stock cartoon figure was the expectant father, pacing the floor and chain smoking in the foyer, while his wife got on with the job in the labour ward. In this case, our wait was two whole days. Late in the night of 9 June, a radio message informed me that a son had been born.

John Frederick Philippi, a delightful little light haired boy had come into the world. His older brothers and sister fell in love with him right away. What we didn't know was that he was merely on loan from heaven.

On Sunday 10 July the following year, we all attended church in a local village. Having run out of boiled water, we were forced to top up with raw water from the village. A bad mistake. Next Wednesday, after an unusually long sleep, he came down with diarrhoea. We gave him some medicine, which seemed to control it, but on Thursday a mild fever developed. We got onto the radio and contacted the hospital at Yagaum, and the diarrhoea seemed over. When it started again on Friday, we commenced him on a sulpha drug, and again called Yagaum for advice. Matters were now getting serious. For most of Saturday morning, the poor little fellow appeared all right, but in the afternoon the diarrhoea reappeared, and by five o'clock he had passed eleven watery stools. This time, we got into the car and drove post haste to Goroka Hospital. At the outpatients' centre, we were met by the same doctor who had delivered him, and she changed the medication. But still the flux continued.

Sunday morning should have been a joyful occasion; it was Theophila's birthday, but John started vomiting. Hurrying back to the hospital, we were met by another doctor, who gave him an injection to ease the vomiting. "Just repeat the medicine until he keeps it down; it's the best one we have. And make sure you keep up his fluids." Then he added the ominous: "There's really nothing more we can do." In retrospect, one wonders why they failed to put him on a drip. Perhaps they were short staffed over the weekend. But he did say, "You can come back tonight for another injection if he keeps vomiting." By this stage, it was clear that John had more output than input.

The family went to church, but John kept passing stool. We therefore called the doctor who had seen him the night before, and were told to bring him back for another injection. Amazingly, as we brought him in, the sister commented, "You know, he really doesn't look sick."

At that point we parted ways. Theophila went to stay in Goroka with our friends, Rev Ralph and Julie Goldhardt, while I took the children home. I also had some more preaching to do, and hoped the congregation would not see how distressed I was. But I did return that evening to check out the situation.

The brownish stool had temporarily ceased. Theophila phoned the doctor, and gave her the news. "In that case," she replied, "come in the morning, and bring a stool." As his mother put the receiver down, John gave a funny look back over his shoulder. "Oh, God!" she thought. "Is he looking into heaven?" John was restless and wriggled constantly throughout the night, as Theophila and the Goldhardts kept vigil. About three in the morning, he took a lot of fluid, then vomited it all up, and passed another stool. At four, they waited no longer.

Rev. Goldhardt rushed them back to the hospital. "Leave him here," the staff insisted; he needed emergency treatment. But at six o'clock the phone rang with the news that our darling, our joy, had just passed away. He had been on this earth only one year, one month, and ten days.

You cannot possibly imagine the emotions of a parent at a time like this unless you yourself have lost a child – and may that never befall you! At first there is an air of unreality; it couldn't possibly have happened so suddenly. Your heart goes numb. And always, the mind tries to find meaning in the tragedy: why? why? as if our children somehow belonged to us, and were not merely held by us in trust. I make no mention of the effect on the other children in the family, whose sense of loss was no less keen for being novel. And yet – and yet – previous generations took it in their stride. They suffered just as severely, but they were under no illusions that life was somehow guaranteed. The literature of previous centuries was replete with the death of children. And it made no difference whether one was high or low. Queen Anne, we know, lost all her seventeen children through miscarriage, stillbirth, or early death. A large history book could be filled with monarchs and aristocrats whose hearts had been broken as sharply as ours. We were living in a country where life was cheap. The wonder was rather that we had lost only one.

Theophila and I washed his little body, and we laid it in the grave that same day. Louis Vogt constructed a little coffin out of plywood. For a land of primitive communications, the news spread with remarkable rapidity. Enaricki, the District President arrived, as did both of our local pastors, and many of the Bena people filed past to view John's body one last time. It was a cheerful funeral, to the extent that any funeral can be called cheerful. Beautiful flowers, even sweet peas, magically appeared at the church. Ralph Goldhardt preached on the twenty-third psalm, and we filled the building with singing,

"Take Thou my hand and lead me,"

and the plaintive words of the children's hymn,

I am Jesus' little lamb,
Ever glad at heart I am;
. . .
Should I not be always glad?
Jesus would not have me sad.
When my days on earth are ended,
By my loving shepherd tended,
In His arms I then shall rest,
There to be forever blest[8].

The coffin was carried to the graveside by four New Guinea pallbearers, one of whom had already borne the coffins of three other children. The casket slipped, and fell crookedly into the hole. They asked us if we wanted it brought out and straightened, but what difference did that make? We let it lie as it fell, and the final prayers were said. One of those looking on had been John's little playmate, Ian Vogt, who later commented, "Mummy, John has gone down to Heaven." So be it.

We later sent away for a bronze plaque bearing the words of Job 1:21: "The Lord gave, and the Lord has taken away. Blessed be the name of the Lord." We have recently heard that, following independence, the cemetery has become overgrown with weeds, and the grave is impossible to find. Which is rather sad.

The following day, many of those who had been unable to attend the funeral at short notice arrived to pay their respects. Many of them wept, and we had the opportunity to tell them that John was with Jesus. His death also gave them the opportunity to witness the dignity with which a Christian faces bereavement. We did not burn the possessions of the deceased, nor cover ourselves with mud for a year, nor cut off an ear, nor

---

[8] *Weil ich Jesus Schäflein bin*, by Henriette von Hayn, translated by William Stevenson, 1871. Hymn no. 602 in the Lutheran Hymnal.

175

the joint of a finger. (Lev. 19:28: "You shall not make any cuttings in your flesh on account of the dead or tattoo any marks upon you: I am the Lord.") When two Christians did arrive bearing heathen mourning marks, I remonstrated with them. But when a third man came to my office smeared with mud – and I must at least give him credit for his act of sympathy – he told me, "See this, the people said I shouldn't put this on, but I'm not a Christian, so I can."

At this point I should add, that we have had so many evil customs come up at this time amongst our Christian people, it was as if the Lord wanted us to set and example for them. In one place the people kept a man after he died in his house for a month without any embalming. In another, a child was near death and the people killed pigs to placate the evil spirits that were killing the child, this amongst Christians! In still another case one of our pastors lost his son of about twenty years, and we heard a lot of talk of sorcery connected with his death. Not only do they disfigure themselves for the dead, but a few years later, we actually met a man who had had his middle finger chopped off because of the loss of a pig! Another custom is that when a person dies, they buy a lot of new clothes, such as laplaps   and bury it with the body, and this may included tinned meat, or even mother's milk in the case of a child. Spoons, plates, and other utensils   are put on the graves of the dead in connection with their spirits. They have such a fear of the spirits of the dead that many of the funeral practices are specifically designed to prevent the ghost from returning to haunt the living. The people truly needed the witness of a Christian burial, and in our meetings with our evangelist and pastors this now began to be stressed. How terrible it must be if, instead of leaving your loved ones to the mercy of God, you live in fear that they will become unquiet spirits prepared to torment you.

Theophila washed our baby's little clothes, and put them away. His passing had left a hole in our daily routine as wide as the emptiness in our hearts. There was quiet where once there had been noise, stillness where once there was bustle. It takes years to get over it.

At the time, we had been unable to contact our families overseas about the disaster, so shortly afterwards, we sent a circular around to all our friends and relations. About five years later, one of the recipients suffered a similar bereavement, so he dug out the letter, read it again, and then wrote to tell us it had aided him in his time of trouble.

Fortunately – if such a word is possibly appropriate – all this happened at a time when we had to be busy. The four day district conference was due just nine days after the funeral, and it was to be held at Bena Bena, so we had to get cracking with the organization. Two cows and six pigs were purchased by the Bena people to add to the sweet potatoes, rice, carrots, pumpkins, and soya beans, for there were two hundred people in attendance most days, increasing to two hundred and forty nine on Sunday. Temporary accommodation had to erected for them, and even then, there was an overflow billeted on the nearby villages. We had to borrow from all our neighbors, while Theophila managed a team of twenty women and four men. The cooking was done in big kettles, in which we also heated water for the laundry. All the time, I was supervising the transport of 44-gallon drums full of water from the stream down below, and chasing the nearby villages for food and firewood. I hardly got to attend a single conference meeting.

To make matters more interesting, on the first night, two strangers sneaked into the village of Hofagayufa in order to practice sorcery. The locals were not amused, and both of them had to run for their lives, even though one of them had been shot four times.

The next month (18 August) I was visiting Kapokamarigi when the Seventh Day Adventist Council announced that the men of Kapokamaragi and Hofagayufa were about to have a battle on the ground between them. An urgent attempt was made to call the police, but when we returned to Kopokamarigi, we discover that four of them were suffering arrow wounds to the arms, and were boasting that they had wounded three of the "enemy": in the eye, chest, and arm. Then the kiap came and rounded them all up. The very next days the Kokinaga and Sigoyas decided to use the land above our place for their public battle. I called the police, who immediately arrived and confiscated all their weapons.

Thank God we now had something to keep our minds occupied!

Time heals all wounds, but leaves the scars. On 21 September 1967, at 1.30 pm, just fourteen months and three days after God took John from us, he gave us a second daughter, Christine Elizabeth as a replacement. At the time, her father was flat on his bed from the result of a recent back injury – and stayed that way for three weeks. At least one member of the family had a chance to rest!

Christine didn't know it, of course, but she had a brand new house to live in, with real wooden walls, ceiling, and verandah. With relief and joy, we had watched it rise out of the ground under the hands of an expert team of builders and carpenters, all of them black. Progress was coming to the land where, twenty years before, I had arrived with a team of builders and carpenters, because there was no-one else qualified for the job.

The dedication was held on 8 July, beginning with a singsing by the carpenters, dressed in western clothing, which lasted all morning. After them came the people of Hofagayufa in all their finery: laplaps and grass skirts about their waists, gleaming kina shells around their necks, and balanced on their heads, gigantic frameworks of wood, covered with white feathers. Not even a brief, sudden downpour could dampen their spirits.

As the day progressed, European friends from as far afield as Goroka, Rintebe, and Asaroka filed in. Even our Seventh Day Adventist neighbors put in an appearance.

At two p.m. the dedication began. Sigayong gave a prayer in Bena and a song. Both district presidents (bishops), Baina the black president, and his white associate, Rev Bamler were present. Baina gave a sermon, after which Kai, the head carpenter opened the door and presented the key to Baina, and then to me. Rev. Bamler came up and said the benediction, and the service ended with a song in Pidgin. Then everyone came in to see the house, and tea, coffee, and cordial were served to the Europeans.

As for our old aluminium house, we watched it being disassembled and loaded onto a truck, with the kitchen on a separate vehicle, thence, presumably, to be taken and reassembled for some lucky, newly arrived missionaries. I hope they appreciated it!

Chapter 11
Good-bye to All That

Our final years in New Guinea were neither boring nor uneventful, but they probably do not merit detailed description. It is the first years of any endeavour which are most interesting, for it is then that most of the new circumstances and experiences occur; the later years are more routine.

Our children were growing up. So was the territory. Increasingly, on circuit, we would see pick and shovel being wielded to link villages by road where once only crude foot trails existed. Increasingly, the vehicles they carried had native drivers. The economic success of the Bena people with coffee growing had lead them to purchase cars and run them in the ground, because their appetite for consumer goods had outpaced their knowledge and interest in maintaining them. The local council was providing roads, schools, village water supplies and similar utilities. Increasingly, the administration was also being performed by black graduates from the government and mission schools. We were seeing more black policemen, and even magistrates. Independence was in the offing. 1968 saw the first ever universal election. Prior to that, not even the white settlers had had any say in the running of the territory.

In a like manner, the missionaries were seeking to work themselves out of a job, and produce a fully self-governing, indigenous church. To this end, every district (other denominations would call them dioceses) was governed by two concurrent presidents – the equivalent of bishops – each appointed for a set term: a district president (black) and a district missionary (white). Baina was our Goroka district president, but on 27 June 1968 District Missionary Bamler went home to Germany on four months' furlough, and Leon was appointed his locum. Of course, it didn't mean that anyone else did *his* job at Bena Bena. It just meant that he was now considered efficient enough to manage two jobs at once.

Meanwhile, our second furlough was coming due. On Thursday 7 November, we were at the village of Sigele, when the evangelist, Totora presented us with going away presents: a bride price arrow for Leon, and for Theophila, the spear used by women to support their men in battle, as explained in the last chapter. For the next couple of weeks, the missionary families invited us to their homes, and the Bena people held special functions for us. Then, on 20th of the month, we all flew out to Australia, where Theophila's parents had again hired a caravan to accommodate us in their back yard. But we stayed only three weeks before heading off to America – this time by air. (How times had changed!)

Our home for the next eight and a half months would be a comfortable two storey brick building in Muscatine, Iowa which Leon's parents had rented for us, and which they had furnished with items   borrowed from all around the community. But the transition was a shock for the children. Nut-brown from the tropical sun – for they had all inherited their mother's olive complexion – and clad only in the light weight garments of the Highlands' cool season, they now faced the ice and snow of the Midwestern winter. But at least they had something for "show and tell" when they walked to school (it was nearby), for we had found termites in the basement where the furnace stood. The owners expressed gratitude of our drawing it to their attention.

At the start of the school day, in their quaint Australian accents, they now exercised their joint citizenship by swearing allegiance "to the flag of the United States, and the Republic for which it stands", instead of singing, "God Save the Queen." But they were in for a bigger culture shock than that. They now found they were supposed to be already familiar with the names, positions, and capitals of forty-eight states instead of the far more convenient six states and two territories, and to know about George Washington and Abraham Lincoln, instead of Captain Cook and Arthur Phillip. And Esther still talks about having stones and insults hurled at her for being a nigger lover. As a native of New Guinea, she found it easier to relate to black people than white, and naturally gravitated to the Negro girls.

She also has straight teeth now. While in America, we took her to a dentist and paid $800 to have them straightened. You have no idea what a colossal sum that was in those days.

We had permitted two months' holiday before Leon's deputation work commenced on 25 January, initially in Muscatine itself and its immediate environs, during school term, but soon further afield. We purchased a Rambler Studbaker, and the advent of the school summer holidays allowed us to strike out further afield – to Leon's old stamping ground of Nebraska, a working holiday for us parents, a complete holiday for the children.

At last, it was time for a joint holiday. One of our many contacts, a Pastor Boyce kindly lent us a camping trailer, complete with a fold-out kitchenette at the back. With the addition of a gas stove and a set of sleeping bags, we were off to South Dakota, Wyoming, and Yellowstone National Park. It was there that Theophila got up close and personal with a hungry grizzly, and was forced to quickly wind up the window against its pig-like snout. From there, we drove to Minnesota, to spend a week at the Hazel Glade Resort at Waukon. Then it was off to Strawberry Point, Iowa because, while still in New Guinea, Leon had accepted a position as chaplain at a youth camp there. Unfortunately, on our first night there it rained cats and dogs, and our huge nylon tent leaked at any point where it got touched. Eventually, we bundled the children off into the car, while we ourselves sat up on the cots under our umbrellas, and tried to sleep that way. But the morning rose bright and clear, and provided a beautiful manifestation of the Midwestern woodlands.

But all good things must come to an end. On 1st September we flew back to Australia. Although our base would be Sydney, the first item on the agenda was to board a train for Brisbane, where we enrolled Peter and Esther at St Peter's

College, Indooroopilly. This Lutheran boarding school had a long and venerable tradition of providing secondary school education for missionary children. It was back to "God Save the Queen", Captain Cook, and eight capital cities, but it also meant expensive school uniforms, the struggle to catch up on a year's syllabus in the last two months of term, getting used to dormitories, absence from family, and comments on their newly acquired American accents.

The family in 1969.
Left to right: Theophila and Peter, Christine, Leon, Esther, and Tim.

In October, Leon gave speeches and slide shows in the Sydney area, but then we purchased yet another automobile, and for the better part of November he was involved in a whistle stop tour of southern New South Wales. Theophila, in the interim, remained in Sydney, where Timothy was also seeking to catch up on the last months of primary school. For all of the children, it was a relief when school ended, and at two p.m. on 30 December, all six of us were back in Goroka.

It was like stamping on an ant nest. The very next Sunday (4 January, 1970) found Leon in the middle of a series of social and family conflicts in the village of Mehewaga. The teacher, Wiwinuc had committed adultery with the Bible schoolteacher at Hofagayufa called Manape. To his own wife, this was the last straw. She claimed that she was alone by herself most of the time, and also that he had kept all of the Christmas wages for himself. So on 3rd December, she had walked out on him – but not before taking a knife, and cutting one of the schoolgirls, Siokie by name, for reasons we failed to record. The result was an on-going court case, and an act of private vengeance, when three men came in and bashed her up.

In another village, Katagu, it was just as bad. The English teacher, Fungkepo and his wife just did not get along. He claimed that she refused to cook for him or wash his clothes, but simply took his keys and ran away with them. Her version was that she did do the cooking, but he wouldn't eat her food, preferring to eat with his parents instead. So, on 19 December he had taken another woman. Now he wanted to get rid of his first wife, despite the fact that she was pregnant, and was demanding the return of the bride price, which came to £25 and five pigs.

In yet another village, a Christian decided to take a second wife, so his first wife, Arari left him and joined up with a man called Sopi. But now he had lost her as well, and so Leon was left to try to pull all the tangled strands together and "straighten it out".

And we'd been back only five days!

The soap opera of Wiwinuc and Manape was far from over. She got pregnant to him - which provoked a fight between her and his legal wife.   In theological terms, this was a "scandal": something which puts the church, and hence the word of God, into disrepute, and serves as a stumbling block for those of weak, or no faith. On 21 July he was discharged from all his duties in the church. There was a fair crowd present at church on 2 August at Hofagayufa, after which the congregation held court. However, both Wiwinuc and Manape expressed their determination to stay together. Wiwinuc's wife then decamped with her own possessions. That evening, the lovers themselves absconded. It turned out they had run away to Lae, and by the time they returned in November, they were (grudgingly) accepted as man and wife.

Meanwhile, on 27 January, we said good-bye to Peter and Esther, who flew out, as unaccompanied minors, to Brisbane, to board again at St Peter's. We would not see them again until the major school holidays. At least, on shorter holidays such as Easter, friends took them into their homes. That is one of the earthly advantages of belonging to the church: you have spiritual brothers and sisters everyone to provide mutual support.

The circuits in February and March painted a dismal picture. In one village, the evangelist explained that there had been no Holy Communion since February 1969, and no church services for the last three months, because of a fight in which nine houses had been burnt down. Although the (white) kiaps were supposed to be keeping the peace, none had been there since the previous October. The previous week, two nearby villages almost went to war, but instead confined themselves to cutting down each other's coffee trees. In the village of Masagu, church services were more regular, but no-one would walk about at night due to an all-pervading fear of sorcery. When Leon got to Orege, he found the situation was grim. Apparently, matters had escalated after someone in Orege had stolen a pig from Safa in 1969. The Safa people retaliated by putting an arrow into an Orege man, but he survived. Then Orege shot a Safa man, who failed to survive. By now, everyone was roaming around with bows and arrows waiting for the next shot to be fired. As a result, the church was a stinking ruin, and all of the Christians had gone bush to live.

After that, things were reasonably quiet until Sunday 19 July. About 6 o'clock that evening, there was a loud commotion in the village of Hofagayufa, next to the mission. Then, at 20 to seven, a band of men from Sigoya set fire to the house of a Hofagayufa man called Seki. Two houses were burnt down, and the flames spread to the home of Sarah, our cook. Leon immediately sent two assistants out to investigate. They returned to announce that a major fight was in progress. Leon therefore jumped into the Land Rover, picked up Stan Thompson, the headmaster at the Seventh Day Adventist school, and then headed for Mohoweto, where he picked up two more S.D.A. workers. Together they raced back to Hofagayufa to calm things down. By then, the battle was over, a lot of people had fled into the bush, and all that was left was to treat the wounded, and try to sort out what had happened.

Detailed questioning thereupon allowed them to piece together a story of intrigue and vengeance which would have scarcely have been out of place in Renaissance Italy or Corsica, but which involved three separate Bena Bena villages. Apparently, when the luluai of Hofagayufa had died, a man called Tutupere had spread a rumour that it was the result of sorcery performed by the men of Kapogu. Whether of not the Kapogus had it in for the luluai, they now had it in for Tutupere. When they tried to shoot him, he ducked, and the arrow hit Akepa, the chairman of the local council. That started it! Akepa's brother was shot in the leg. Buff, the translator got it in the hand. One of the Kapogus also received arrows in both his thigh, and the right side of his back. Leon drove the three casualties to Goroka for treatment.

Meanwhile, since Akepa came form Sigoya, his fellow villagers had got into the act, and fired Seki's house. A gang of

Sigoyas now descended on the mission station looking for Hofagyufa people to shoot and, their quest unsuccessful, returned to Sigoya. After we had waited nearly three hours, the police finally arrived - two to Hofagayufa, and two to Sigoya, and stayed all night. Come the morning, a new batch of arrow victims was brought forth for medical treatment: six from Sigoya, four from Hofagayufa, one from Kapogu, plus a schoolboy who had an arrow graze his head. Those still in one piece were dragged into court at 11.30 the same morning. We heard that word had gone out that, if Akepa were to die of his wound, the Sigoyas were planning to kill Pewefa, our teacher at Hofagayufa.

Fortunately, that failed to eventuate, but five days later twelve more people from Hofagayufa were shot. And all this just a short drive from one of the biggest towns and administrative centres in the Highlands, in a country just five years off independence!

A couple of weeks later, on Friday, 7 August, Peter and Esther flew home for the school holidays. The nearby Seventh Day Adventist native boarding school was still in session, and when we heard it was offering piano lessons the following Tuesday, it was thought Esther and Timothy might benefit. They were then aged thirteen and ten respectively, but both were well familiar with the area, and a walk of a few miles down a narrow bush trail had never been considered an issue in the past. However, that day, we were shocked to see Esther come running back to the mission station at a furious pace, disheveled, frantic, and shaking with emotion. Her brother brought up the rear, in a similar state of distress. Between sobs, and gasps for breath, they blurted out an alarming story. As it turned out, they had been nonchalantly wending their way homewards, Tim being well in front, and playing with a stick. Suddenly, an older teenager sprang out of the kunai grass and threw his arms around Esther, his right hand still grasping a spear. "*Yu kam puspus long mi!*" he cried ("You come and have sex with me!") as he sought to drag her into the undergrowth.

Screaming at the top of her lungs, Esther turned against her attacker. At that, her plucky younger brother came charging back and threw himself into the fray. Two against one was a bit much for the assailant. Breaking free, Esther fled down the trail. Her opponent then took after Timothy, who bolted into the undergrowth. The schoolboy followed, only to fall right over his quarry. In the confusion, Tim burst back on to the trail, and raced after his sister. Neither of them drew breath until they were safe at the station.

This was too much! Witchcraft and warfare were one thing, but up to now no-one had ever dared lay hands on a member of the family. Quickly bundling Esther and Timothy into the vehicle, Leon drove down the road to the school, whereupon Stan Thompson, the head, had a roll call and made the boys line up. Walking down the line, Esther examined every face, rejecting each in turn. Halfway down, they saw some young fellow trying to skulk away. "That's the one!" cried Esther, as Stan dragged him out. "Yes, that's him!" added Tim, in confirmation.

"No, no!" he cried. It wasn't him. He had been with the other boys and girls all along. It was a bare faced lie. The marks of Esther's fingernails on his face still glared as testimony against him. Well, asked Stan, when he called the others over, could anyone back him up? They couldn't. On the contrary, one of the boys came forth and reported that he had seen the troublemaker follow the water and skulk off into the undergrowth. Confronted with two witnesses, and a scratched cheek, the culprit broke down and confessed.

It was now six o'clock. At seven, Stan brought him down to our place, and we took him to the Goroka police station. He confessed once again, and they locked him up. Justice moved fast in New Guinea in those days. At ten the next day he faced the court. Thankfully, Esther didn't need to testify, because he pleaded guilty. He was given a one month suspended sentence, with parole for one year. In other words, he got away scot free! His only "punishment" was to be required to obey the law for one year – which is what we all have to do! That should have taught him a lesson!

To this day, Esther will not walk in the bush by herself, and is even on the alert when walking alone through suburban streets.

Sadly, Peter and Esther were forced to return to Brisbane all too soon. A couple of weeks later, *they* had some surprise visitors. Their Aunt Lois Philippi had just become Mrs Mike Cipalo of Chicago. Normal Americans honeymoon at Niagara Falls, but they had chosen New Guinea. But first, they had a short stopover in Brisbane, where they called on Esther and Peter, and treated them to dinner at Lennon's Hotel, in a restaurant far swankier than they, or we, could ever afford, and presented with the choice of a live lobster from a tank.

It was with eager anticipation that we drove out to meet them at the Goroka airport. Young Timothy sat in the back with the newlyweds, but he could not take his eyes off his new uncle's shiny bald dome. Eventually, it got took much, and he blurted out: "What happened to your hair?" (New Guinea males, it should be noted, occasionally suffer a receding hairline. They may end up, so to speak, with a fairly high forehead. But, like the Australian Aborigines, they practically never go completely bald.)

We set them up in the clay brick house we used as an office for circuit work when it wasn't doing duty as a guesthouse. The only drawback was that it was furnished with a chamber pot instead of an indoor toilet. Every morning, an embarrassed bride used to carry it outside, discretely concealed by a bag bearing the logo of Marshall Fields, the most prominent department store in Chicago.

They came on picnics with us. We let them experience the routine of church services and circuits. They gazed with new eyes on things which had become commonplace with us –

189

things like altars of woven pitpit, the use of Coke bottles as vases for the flowers, the way the men and women sat on opposite sides of the church, a woman in church suckling a baby on one breast and a piglet on the other. They were presented with gifts of bows and arrows.

At one point, Lois objected when Leon insisted she wear a dress for church, but proprieties had to be observed. The congregation probably would not have objected if she had arrived topless, but slacks or shorts on a woman was a definite no-no. Of course, it went without saying that the route to be negotiated was just a simple bush track. When attempting to descend a steep embankment, she lost her step, skidded down on her skirted posterior, and required the assistance of Theophila to remove the gravel and splinters from her stern. It didn't do the dress any good, either.

A week after their arrival, Mike accompanied Leon on one of his visits, this time by road. However, he was forced to wait in the vehicle while his new brother-in-law conducted business inside. And he waited. And waited. And all the time he was thinking: here I am in the middle of the jungle, stuck in some unknown village full of savages of whose customs and attitudes I know nothing, and I have no idea what is going on, how long I am going to have be here, or who could even speak enough English to tell me, if I were game enough to ask. At last, with the shadows of dusk lengthening, Leon returned. He explained that the native pastor, Jatefa had been beaten up in a fight between the villages of Kenimaro and Mohoweto and, in a separate incident, members of two other villages had had thirteen arrows shot into them. Mike may have been unfamiliar with such incidents back home, but they took a long time to "straighten out".

Lois and Mike's visit had been one of the highlights of the year, and a delightful counterbalance to the drama of the previous month. It was sad when they had to go, after only twelve days. Of course, if they had stayed another couple of weeks, they would have heard more of the type of event they never encounter at home. Pastor Hojafa, of Sigoya, had been walking to another village for a church dedication when a man from a third village kindly presented him with some betel nut. He had been happily chewing away when his wife, somehow sensing danger, cried out that it was poisoned, and told him to spit it out. Shortly afterwards, he got violently sick, so he induced himself to vomit with a mixture of kerosene and hair oil. For nearly a week he lay gravely ill, and fears were held for his survival. For several nights his father was awakened by mysterious knockings on his door, which was interpreted as Hojafa's spirit announcing his imminent death. We didn't hear about it until a week later, by which time he had recovered.

The following month, October, the two villages closest to the mission station, Hofagayufa and Kapokamarigi went to war. (This was getting to be monotonous!) As was frequently the case, the issue was land. You will remember from the last chapter, that the two villages were separated by an hour and a quarter of rugged terrain. Nevertheless, the site where Kapokamarigi had erected a fence was disputed territory, and that brought Hofagayofa out in force. As you will also have gathered by this stage, a typical confrontation involves both sides standing their ground, yelling and shouting, and brandishing their weapons. Unless one side then withdraws, it progresses to the second stage, where weapons are discharged, and after a few casualties on one or both sides, one or both sides withdraws. Astute readers will note similarities to the behaviour of teenage gangs in the slums of our own cities, and bands of chimpanzees in the African jungle. Human nature hasn't advanced all that much.

In this instance, the fight was halted by the intervention of a courageous church elder named Irakowe, who stood his ground as a series of arrows were fired at him. In hindsight, one suspects that they merely wished to frighten him, because none of them connected. If so, they were sadly mistaken, and when they saw that he meant business, they eventually dispersed. Irakowe then picked up three of the arrows and went home. He was another of those forgotten indigenous saints who have done so much for the advancement of this wild country.

The following day, Thursday, Leon was on his way to a third village to give a sermon when he saw that the Hofagayufas and Kapokamarigis were at it again. Hundreds of people were lined up for a fight. He therefore drove to the main road and sent a note to the police, By then it was 8.40 a.m. Eventually, he made his way to Kapokamarigi and discussed the matter with the local (native) teacher, who promptly went to the police station. At last, four policemen came and "sang out" to the population, but didn't go down to where the fighting was. Nevertheless, their presence probably had an inhibitory effect on the warriors. Leon and his companions talked with both sides for two hours, until the more recalcitrant members simply went home in high dudgeon.

The day after that, Leon consulted the kiap and the police in Goroka. The police spokesman shook his head. "Unfortunately," he explained, "there is really not much we can do at this stage. We'd like to keep the peace, but we can't be everywhere at once. We can only wait until a real fight breaks out again. Then we can go in and arrest the perpetrators."

The kiap thanked Leon for the information. "Your intervention probably saved a few lives," he said, "but it was a darned stupid thing to do. Anyhow, I'll deal with it from here on. You keep out of it."

With the weight of all the colonial responsibility on his shoulders, he then went to the leaders of the two villages and, metaphorically speaking, bashed their heads together. When Leon returned a week later, the Kapokamarigis were busy erecting a fence, while the Hofagayufas watched from a distance, their bows and arrows lying on the ground. Even that did not satisfy the kiap, and after a lapse of ten days, the Kapokamarigis were observed cutting the barbed wire down. They had bought it for $130 – a fearful sum in that area – and gained nothing except a fine of $100 for their trouble.

It would be nice to say that that was the end of the matter, but almost exactly a month later, the fence went up again. On the third day, one of the Hofagayufa elders told them: "We're going to cut the wire. If you want to fight, then fight. Your people will die, and so will some of ours. Don't tell the police!"

So the next day they fought. The elder's brother was killed, and quite a few people were wounded. Then the police came and rounded up the lot, as they said they would. After that, peace reigned, but the following January, Kapokamarigis were seen farming the land they had effectively won in the conflict. Like the slumland gangs and the chimpanzees, the band with the most persistence eventually gains the ground.

Life settled down, and 1970 faded into 1971. The children were all present for the Christmas holidays. Esther then returned to St Peter's, but the principal had written to us that Peter was not "academically suited" to the school, so we enrolled him at Asaroka. Since the school was on the other side of Goroka, we dipped into the missionary support network once again, and our friends, the Tscharkes agreed to board him throughout the week. He was thus able to return home on weekends. Poor Peter! No-one could predict that his adult life would be marred by the curse of schizophrenia, and his later years with emphysema. Shortly before his fifty-sixth birthday, he passed away in his chair.

The Bena Bena district was now peaceful. Admittedly, in August eighteen houses were burned down in a couple of distant villages and the perpetrators thrown into jail, but apart from that, our diaries reveal no more fighting. Either the warring villagers had learned their lesson, or the authorities were more successful at suppressing it. The most dramatic event in the first half of the year was the earthquake. We had been used to tremors in the past; New Guinea is on a tectonic zone, and one gets accustomed to the mountains shrugging their shoulders at irregular intervals. But the one that struck at

5.10 am on Friday 12 February rated six on the Richter scale. Even so, it didn't disturb the tenor of our activities. But at 8.14 that Sunday we were woken by a tremendous shaking, and rushed out to see the ground heaving like waves in the sea. Throughout the day, the jolts continued, the big one in the afternoon being particularly frightening. Our water tank, which was four rings high, almost toppled over, and with mute horror, we watched the house shake like a leaf in a high wind, and a series of waves pass through the earth, as on a wind swept beach. It then settled down, and we hoped it was all over, but at intervals throughout the night, we would wake with the impression that the earth was moving, like a sleeper whose chest rises and falls with his shallow breathing.

We heard later that the epicentre had been Madang. The cable linking New Guinea to Australia had been broken in five places. The flexible native huts, of course, suffered harm, but there was substantial damage in Madang. On nearby Karkar Island, the coast near the medical centre subsided to such an extent that palm trees twenty metres high were left with only their tops above water.

The second dramatic event occurred on 18 August, at a quarter past two. Theophila was taking the Land Rover into town, four year old Christine in the front seat, and four of the local natives in the back. They had purchased some black dolls from a store, had dressed then in New Guinean fashion, and were planning to sell them to the tourists. Coming down the Mohoweto hill, Theophila tried to apply the brakes. They failed. In desperation, she struggled to maintain control of the vehicle, which careered wildly down the rough terrain, and turned over three times. When the dust had settled, her left arm was found to be broken right next to the shoulder blade. One of the New Guineans required stitches, but the others, including, thankfully, our young daughter, were more or less unscathed. Considering that these were the days before seat belts, it can only be viewed as remarkable.

It was also, coincidentally, the day after Leon ended his

second stint as district missionary, for the new DM, Pastor David Tuff had been absent for four and a half months. Where this would all have ended is anyone's guess. If the church were treated as any ordinary occupation, this would have been considered a major career move, an indication that he was being groomed for leadership. Certainly, although the country and the church were drifting towards independence, the field was still wide open, and ready for sowing. We were happy and fulfilled in our work. The people wanted us, and needed us. We could have stayed for years. There was only a single fly in the ointment: the children's education.

It was not a problem unique to missionaries. Virtually every white family, whether in the church, administration, or plantations, faced the same issue. Nor was it unique to New Guinea. The literature of India and Africa spell out a sorry litany of children exiled to the mother country for years on end simply for the sake of education. The life of a colonialist was not all beer and skittles.

We had tried home schooling by correspondence, and that had been a failure. Right now, Timothy was still sitting forlorn and alone at the "bus stop" store, waiting for the milk van to bring him to the classroom after all the other children had started. In a couple of years, we would need to find a high school for him. Peter was now in exile five days out of seven, and Esther three months out of every four. And when they finished, where would they go, and what would they do? Then, in a year or two, the whole circus was going to start again for Christine. It was for this reason that we decided to leave New Guinea.

The church, to its credit, gave its support. The same was not true for everyone. Theophila's parents said, in effect: "You have been called for life. The captain cannot leave his ship." But in this life, no-one is indispensable except a spouse or a parent. God could easily find service for us elsewhere, and He could easily replace us on the mission field.

The decision also brought to the fore an issue which had

been on the back burner for the last twenty years: nationality. When two marry from different nations, in the end, one allegiance must prevail. If there had been a place for Leon in the U.S. church, no doubt we would all consider ourselves Americans today. However, a brief enquiry ascertained that there were two hundred surplus Lutheran pastors in America. On 19 August, therefore – coincidentally, the day after Theophila's accident – Leon applied for Australian citizenship. There would be no problem, the reply came, provided he had employment lined up in the country beforehand.

In the Lutheran church, when a congregation needs a pastor, they put out a "call", mediated by their president. Leon therefore asked the Australian general president, Dr. Lohe for a call, but nothing eventuated. He then took the advice of Bishop Kuder, and wrote to the Queensland district president, Pastor F. Schmidt. After that, things started to move quickly. Within a fortnight - on 26 November, to be precise - we received a call to the parish of Ropely, near Gatton in southeast Queensland. We accepted it by mail the following day. On 10 December, we drove down to the Goroka Court House and, at 1.30 p.m., Leon and Peter took the oath of allegiance to the Queen. (It is only fair to point out, however, that, in Peter's case, this was unnecessary; like his younger siblings, he had dual citizenship. Also, because he was a minor, the U.S. authorities refused to accept his renunciation of citizenship. Presumably, if he had decided to settle in the U.S., as his brother, Tim later did, they would have to take him in.)

So it was, on 7 January 1972 the six of us stood at the airport in Goroka for the last time, with all the complex feelings of anticipation and nostalgia of those who have ended a long chapter of their lives, and are about to commence a new. Images pressed around us of all that had gone before: green jungle and swollen rivers, churches with woven walls, malaria, leprosy, and the grave of a child, witchcraft, war parties, native feasts and festivals, the sound of drums and conch shells. And smiling and waving through them all moved an army of friends:

the mutual support of missionaries, and the native clergy and evangelists, whose need for our tutelage was more than balanced by their loyalty to us and their devotion to God – the fellowship of the saints, both black and white, in a land struggling to rise out of savagery.

As the plane rose into the air, and the clouds and green mountains stretched out below us, we were only half aware that we were watching the end of an era – two eras, in fact: the golden age of colonialism, and the classic missionary experience. Papua New Guinea is now an independent nation – badly governed, to be true, but nevertheless independent, and still democratic. Missionaries still occasionally visit the country, but when they do, it is as assistants to the national church. The fact is, Papua New Guinea is now at the same stage as our own homelands were after their initial conversion well over a thousand years ago. Now, as it was then, sorcery, superstition, and dark pagan practices are almost universal, and the veneer of Christianity is even thinner than in Australia. Nevertheless, at census time, 96 per cent of the population declares its membership of some Christian denomination – one in five of them Lutheran. The seed which fell on good soil has borne fruit – some thirty-, some sixty-, and some a hundred-fold. To have taken part in the sowing had been a blessed calling.

We have never been back to New Guinea. However, it has seldom been far from our hearts – and the feeling may be mutual. "You'd be surprised," a visitor from Begesin told us, "how many people there are named Philippi in your honour." And, every year, whenever possible, we used to attend a reunion of the old hands of the mission field, and renewed old friendships. We have discovered, as have many others before and since, that you may leave New Guinea but, if your stay has been at all substantial, New Guinea never leaves you. Indeed, if you have given it the labours of your youth, and the raising of your family, it becomes the defining experience of your life.

The Authors

Leon and Theophila served as pastor and wife in various parishes in Queensland, especially in the southeast, until the late 1990s, and after that undertook relief work in other parishes on a part time basis for many more years.

They had been married for 63 years when Theophila passed away peacefully in 2017. Leon now resides in a nursing home on the Darling Downs.

Malcolm Smith has lived all his life in Australia, and therefore should not be confused with the expat businessman and politician in Papua New Guinea. Born in 1949, he is a qualified zoologist, a retired public servant, the author of several books, and the husband of the Philippis' elder daughter, Esther.

Made in the USA
Middletown, DE
20 December 2020